AVOCADO OBSESSION

AVOCADO OBSESSION

50+ Creative Recipes to Take Your Love of Avocados to the Next Level

Lauren Paige Richeson

Illustrations by Laura Greenan

ROCKRIDGE
PRESS

For general information on our other products and services or to obtain technical support, please contact our Customer Care Department within the United States at (866) 744-2665, or outside the United States at (510) 253-0500.

Rockridge Press publishes its books in a variety of electronic and print formats. Some content that appears in print may not be available in electronic books, and vice versa.

Interior and Cover Designer: Erik Jacobsen
Art Producer: Tom Hood
Editor: Gleni Bartels
Production Editor: Mia Moran
Illustrations @ Laura Greenan 2020

ISBN: Print 978-1-64739-627-5
eBook 978-1-64739-628-2
R0

For the adventurous.
As Mark Twain said, "Why not go out on a limb?
That's where the fruit is."

CONTENTS

INTRODUCTION

I like to think of avocados as the A-list celebrity of the produce aisle: They're temperamental, a lot of them can be found in California, they're rich (with nutrients)—no wonder so many people have become obsessed! It's a challenge to scroll through any social media feed without encountering at least one. They boost smoothies, steaks, even cocktails and desserts with their healthy, delicious creaminess. So it was only a matter of time until someone gave these glamorous green fruits the recognition they deserved with a cookbook dedicated entirely to them.

I'm Lauren Paige (LP to my friends), a self-taught home chef, recipe creator, and food photographer. I've spent years studying international cuisines and health and wellness. I'm also an adventurer and avocado obsessive. From my very first avocado slice, it was true love at first creamy bite. Since then, I've traveled the world and tasted hundreds of dishes, but my favorite flavors always come back to the versatile and velvety avocado.

For those who are already avocado aficionados, chances are you have your go-to guacamole and toast recipes. My mission here is to go above and beyond so you can enhance your avocado repertoire. From elegant recipes (like Mediterranean-Style Chicken Breasts with Tangy Avocado Tapenade on page 80) to effortless ones (try the Green Goddess Smoothie Bowl on page 14), we will slice, dice, puree, and sauté our way to dishes that are creative, delicious, and packed with flavors that are avo this world!

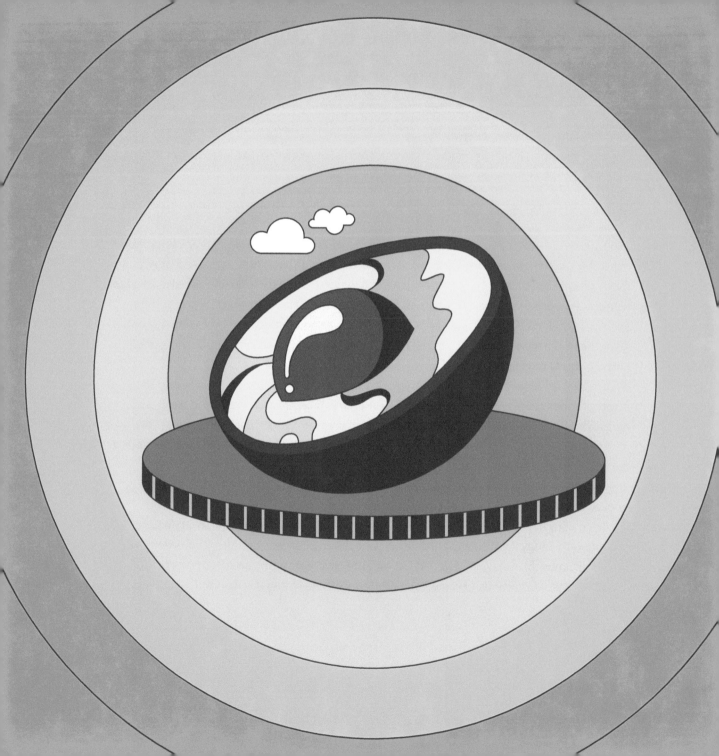

Chapter 1

Welcome to the wonderful world of avocados! We're about to embark on an avo-adventure, exploring fun new ways to enjoy your favorite food. If you feel like you've hit guac bottom, I've got some fresh ideas to get you moving in the ripe direction. First, we'll get to the pit of things and dig into some facts, figures, and fundamentals of our green supreme. So grab a lime, and let's move fast. We're working on avocado time.

Your Obsession Is Totally Justified

Avocados, while loved, have long been misunderstood. Under that tough shell and inside that hard core, they're really just a soft fruit. Yes, a fruit. Botanically speaking, avocados are actually just large berries. Is your mind blown? Avocado worship started way before the long lines at Trader Joe's. The first carbon pit-print dates back to the Aztecs in 10,000 B.C.E. Native to the warm climates of Central America, the creamy green goodness has now been spread on toasts across the globe.

Any way you cut it (on page 7 I'll tell you how), avocados have earned their way to the top of the food-trend chain by being a powerhouse of nutrients and healthy fats, having a wide culinary range, and simply tasting *really* good. Avocados hold the crown when it comes to "superfoods," a group of so-named fruits and veggies that abound in minerals, vitamins, and antioxidants and are thought to have healing powers. (Sorry, apples, looks like it's an avocado a day now!)

Hass for Thought: Avocados are filled with omega-3 fatty acids and are a natural source of vitamin E, both of which are great for boosting brain power.

They Love You Back: Avocados are one of the fattiest plant foods in the world, but worry not. They're full of monounsaturated oleic acid, a heart-healthy fatty acid that has been shown to reduce cholesterol and fight heart disease.

Delicious and Nutritious: Avocados are loaded with over 20 different vitamins and minerals, including magnesium, copper, iron, zinc, and vitamins A, B_1, B_2, and B_3. They have almost twice as much potassium as bananas!

Clear Eyes, Full Bellies: Avocados are high in antioxidants such as lutein and zeaxanthin, which promote eye health and protect against conditions like cataracts.

Fiber Wonder-full: Avocados are filled with fiber. Just one provides your daily dose of this important nutrient that's good for your metabolism and blood sugar levels.

There's More than Just Hass

A trip down the local produce aisle only gives us a small glimpse into the avocado options the world has to offer. Avocados come in all sorts of sizes and flavors, and while they may look similar, every avo is not the same. Let's take a look at this fruity family tree.

Bacon: Not to be confused with your favorite breakfast side, this avocado has a lighter taste than other varieties and is identifiable by its pale yellow-green skin. You can find it in the winter months from November to March.

Choquette: Large and in charge, the Choquette from Florida is known for being one of the biggest of the end-of-summer bunch. It can weigh up to two pounds and has silky flesh that seems to bleed a lime green juice when cut.

Fuerte: The Fuerte, which means "strong" in Spanish, is a mid-August through October California favorite. It has a perfect pear shape with a creamy flavor similar to a hazelnut.

Hass: The Beyoncé of avocados! It's the most popular variety, grown in sunny California. It's available all year round and has a buttery, nutty flavor and oval shape.

Mexicola Grande: Small but beautiful, the deceptively named Mexicola Grande hails from California and is known for its glistening, easy-to-peel black skin and slightly sweet and juicy insides. Find it from August through October.

A California mailman and amateur horticulturist named Rudolph Hass grew the first Hass avocado tree and patented it in 1935.

Obsessing Sustainably

With the surge in demand for this silky fruit, avocado farming has been linked to deforestation, endangering wildlife, and water shortages in Central and South America. While getting your guac fix is important, there are a few things you can do to help offset your avo-impact.

Knowing when and where to buy avocados is vital to making sure we obsess ethically. Buy in season, seek out varieties that are grown domestically in Florida and California, and, when possible, opt for certified-organic avocados to help ensure you're making the most environmentally sound choice.

If you need a jump start, the list on the previous page is full of domestically grown varieties and gives insight into their growing seasons.

 Avocados weren't available in the United States until the 1950s. They rose to popularity in Florida, California, and Hawaii before making their way to the mainstream.

How to Buy an Avocado

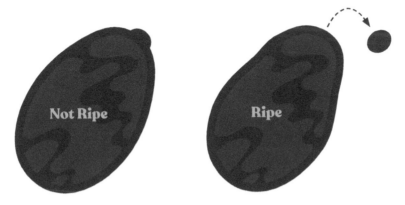

It's no secret that avocados don't age well. It seems like they go from rock hard to ripe to rotten in the blink of an eye. Here are some simple tricks to guarantee you'll always grab an avocado that's guac-ready.

Picking the perfect avocado varies by type, so the first step is to know what's in season. Most avocados change from a dark green to a black/brown when ripe, but others, like the Bacon, may keep their light green hue, so be avo-ware of what you're looking for.

From there, things start to get a little handsy. By giving the avocado a light squeeze, you should be able to tell its ripeness. A ripe avocado will feel slightly soft to the touch but not mushy. Keep patting down the produce aisle until you find one that's a bit pliable and heavy for its size. If you're not into feeling up your fruit, you can always try the navel test: Look for the little button on the avocado where it was picked from the stem. If you can pick the navel off easily, it's ripe and ready to eat.

 Turn an overripe avo into a moisturizing hair mask: Combine half an avocado with one egg yolk, and massage the mixture into your scalp and hair. Rinse it off after 5 minutes and shampoo and condition as usual.

But I Need My Avocado NOW!

So you've got a recipe that calls for avocados, but the only ones you can find are days away from being anything short of a softball. Hass no fear, we've all been there! Here are some popular remedies for what to do when you just need it *now* and tips for what to do if you've missed that elusive ripeness sweet spot.

Use the magic of science. The most reliable Hass hack sounds like it's straight out of a seventh-grade science book: Place the avocado in a brown paper bag with another piece of fruit (an apple or banana). This speeds up the fruit's production of ethylene gas, which naturally promotes ripening. When sealed and stored at room temperature, this method can soften the stiffest of avocados in 1 to 3 days. The more fruit you add, the faster your avocados will ripen. You can also add a small layer of flour to the bag to seal all the gas in.

Wrap the avocado in foil and bake it in the oven. Some swear by this trick, and while it does appear to ripen an avocado in about an hour, the taste and texture tend to miss the mark for direct consumption. I suggest using it if you're in the mood for a creamier smoothie or want to use your avocado for baking.

But what if you've waited too long and now you've got a mushy mess on your hands?

There are a few ways to save your snack from going to the avocado graveyard.

Resuscitate with citrus. If your avocado is just beginning to brown, you can bring it back to life with a sprinkle of fresh citrus juice.

Multipurpose reincarnation. You can still reap all the benefits, even if an avocado is past its prime. An overripened avocado can add creaminess and nutrients to a smoothie (page 109) or salad dressing (page 54).

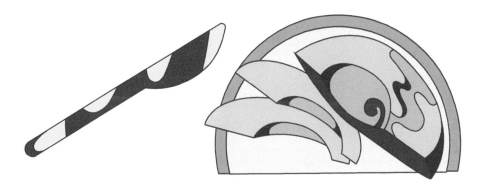

How to Cut an Avocado (Without Going to the ER)

Slicing into an avocado isn't brain surgery, but it can be dangerous if you're not careful. With a little bit of patience, finesse, and a sharp knife, you'll soon be enjoying your avocado, injury free.

1. Using a clean dish towel, securely hold the avocado vertically in the palm of one hand. With a sharp knife, slowly slice vertically down the center into the avocado until the knife hits the pit.

2. Rotate the fruit with your towel-covered hand while keeping the knife steady in the other until you've cut around the entire avocado.

3. Holding the cut avocado in the palm of one hand, use your other hand to twist and rotate the two halves apart.

4. Make a nest with the towel on a stable, flat surface. Put the pitted half of the avocado in the nest, and hold it securely in place. Very carefully tap the blade-edge of the knife into the pit. Twist the knife, and then lift straight up to remove it.

5. Tap the knife on the side of a bowl or carefully grasp the pit with the towel to free it from the knife.

If you're still not completely confident in your knife skills, fear not! There are now special "avocado tools" on the market that can help you safely peel, pit, and slice without the use of a sharp object.

How to Store an Avocado

Store any unripe avocados you don't need right away at room temperature. Make sure to keep an eye on them, though. You don't want to miss your window of avo-tunity! If your avocado is already ripe, simply place the whole fruit in the refrigerator. This will slow the aging process and buy you a few more days.

If you've somehow managed to not eat a whole avocado in one sitting, *bravocado*! For those rare occasions, here are some tips to save that coveted other half, which ultimately means saving some money.

Citrus juice: Remove the pit and coat the flesh in fresh lemon or lime juice, wrap it tightly in plastic wrap, and place it in the fridge. This should last about 2 to 3 days.

Water: An even easier method is to submerge your avocado in water. Place it flesh-side down in a container with an airtight lid, cover, and place it in the fridge. This will keep the avocado from turning brown for about another 2 days.

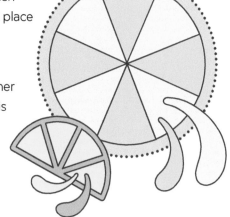

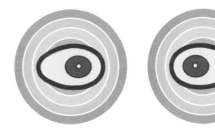

Avoca-Do & Avoca-Don't

DO: Freeze your fruits.

I feel strongly that you should never let a Hass (or a Bacon or a Fuerte . . .) go to waste. While the texture won't be the same after thawing, it'll be perfect as the base for guacamole (page 100), dressings (page 54), and smoothie bowls (page 14).

To freeze: Slice the avocado in half, pit, and peel, then brush with citrus juice and wrap tightly in plastic wrap. Or you can mash your avo with a bit of citrus juice. Store both versions in freezer-safe resealable bags, squeezing out as much air as possible. Let thaw before using.

DON'T: Discard your pits and peels.

Here are a few ways to not let any of the avocado go to waste:

Sprout it: A few toothpicks, a glass of water, an avocado pit, and some sunshine are all you need to get avocado greenery growing!

Tea party: Avocado seeds are packed with antioxidants, and when crushed and soaked in hot water, they become a tummy-soothing tea.

Eco dishware: Use your peels to make cute cups to serve your favorite avocado dishes, like Kickin' Avocado Chicken Salad (page 56).

Your New Favorite Avocado Creations

From breakfast to dinner to dessert to drinks, this book has a recipe for every guac-asion. With a few spins on the classics and some taste-bud-blowing avocado creations, every page is filled with delicious dishes that are Hass-olutely avo this world! Did you ever think the summer would find you licking an avocado-filled ice pop (page 110)? How about crunching on some chips made not from potatoes but from avocado (page 32)?

Each recipe has handy labels so you know just what kind of dish you're dipping into, including **Dairy-Free**, **Gluten-Free**, **Nut-Free**, **Vegan**, **Vegetarian**, and **30 Minutes or Less** (especially good for avocados on the brink of going bad). When dealing with allergens, be sure to read your ingredient labels carefully, and use your best judgment. Throughout, I have labeled recipes containing coconut as "Nut-Free." While allergic reactions have been documented, most people with tree nut allergies can safely eat coconut. However, if you are allergic to tree nuts, talk to your allergist before adding coconut to your diet.

I've also included all sorts of tips and tricks so you can switch, swap, and remix these recipes to fit in your kitchen. And for those of you, like me, who just can't escape avocado toast (and don't want to), I've indulged this obsession and included some unique twists on the trend at the end of almost every chapter.

A heads-up! Keep in mind that when creating these recipes, I mostly stuck to my all-time number one avo, the Hass, which usually weighs about 6 ounces for a medium-size fruit. If your avocados are smaller or larger, you might need to use more or fewer than the amount indicated.

And with that, let's embark on our avocado journey.

 Each year on Super Bowl Sunday, almost 105 million pounds of avocados are consumed.

Chapter 2

Green Goddess Smoothie Bowl

MAKES 2 smoothie bowls / **PREP TIME:** 5 minutes

If your body is a temple, this is one way to prevent ruin. This gorgeous green smoothie is packed with creamy avocado and fresh fruits and veggies. The healthy fat and protein-rich greens from the avocado and spinach, the anti-oxidant and immune-boosting citrus, and the detoxifying ginger and cucumber promise to keep you going all day long.

1 medium avocado, pitted and peeled

1 (2-inch) piece fresh ginger, unpeeled

2 cups coconut water, plus more as needed

1 handful baby spinach

1 medium banana

½ green apple, cored and cut into slices

½ medium cucumber

½ lemon, peeled and seeded

½ lime, peeled and seeded

5 to 6 fresh mint leaves

2 tablespoons flaxseed, plus more for topping

1 teaspoon bee pollen, for topping (optional)

1. In a blender, combine the avocado, ginger, coconut water, spinach, banana, apple, cucumber, lemon, lime, mint, and flaxseed, and pulse on high until completely smooth. Add more coconut water to achieve the consistency you prefer.

2. Top with more flaxseed and bee pollen, if using.

 For a sweeter take, use apple juice instead of coconut water or add a touch of honey.

 Use the bee pollen, which you can find at health food and specialty stores, and receive an influx of all the essential amino acids, fatty acids, and enzymes your body could possibly need. Cholesterol-lowering acai berries or adaptogens like maca or reishi for gut health also make tasty and healthy toppings.

Creamy Banana-and-Avocado Overnight Oats

SERVES 4 / PREP TIME: 5 minutes, plus 4 hours (or overnight) to chill

This is a super-delicious breakfast twist on the Vietnamese avocado-based dessert sinh tố bo, which translates to "butter fruit smoothie." These sweet and creamy oats will boost your energy and keep you full, and they are a great way to use that overripe avocado on your counter. To add crunch and texture, I like to top my bowl with cacao nibs, coconut flakes, or granola before serving.

1 medium avocado, pitted, peeled, and diced

1 small banana

1 cup coconut milk

3 tablespoons honey

Pinch sea salt

2 cups rolled oats

1. In a large bowl, combine the avocado and banana and mash until smooth. Add the coconut milk, honey, salt, and oats. Stir together until well mixed.

2. Divide the mixture evenly among 4 containers with tight-fitting lids, and refrigerate for 4 hours (or overnight) before serving. They will last for 2 days in the refrigerator.

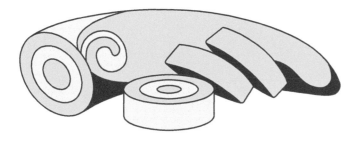

Savory Egg-and-Salmon Avo Oatmeal

SERVES 1 / PREP TIME: 5 minutes / COOK TIME: 10 minutes

Have you ever tried savory oatmeal? This delicious combination of avocado, egg, and salmon comes together to give your old standby a serious upgrade. Once you try this version, you'll never go back to plain old maple and brown sugar again. I've written this recipe to serve one, but it's easy to scale depending on how much you need. If you're feeling extra decadent, top the bowl with Avocado Hollandaise (page 104).

3 cups water, divided

½ cup rolled oats

Sea salt

1 large egg

½ medium avocado, pitted, peeled, and sliced

3 ounces sliced smoked salmon

4 to 5 cherry tomatoes, diced

Freshly ground black pepper

2 tablespoons grated Parmesan cheese

Chopped fresh dill, for topping

1. In a medium pot, bring 1 cup of water to a boil over medium heat. Add the oats and a pinch of salt. Cover, reduce the heat, and simmer for 5 minutes. Remove the pot from the heat and set aside.

2. In a small saucepan, bring the remaining 2 cups of water to a boil. In a small bowl, crack the egg, being careful not to break the yolk. With a spoon, stir the water in a circular motion to create a tornado effect, gently pour the egg into the hot water, and continue to stir the water around the egg. Reduce the heat to low and cook, stirring, for 3 minutes. With a slotted spoon, remove the egg from the pot and set it aside.

3. Place the oatmeal in a deep bowl and top it with the egg, avocado, smoked salmon, and tomatoes. Season with salt and pepper and top with the Parmesan and dill.

 Don't feel like poaching an egg? Soft-boiled, fried, or scrambled eggs work, too.

 Rolled oats absorb more liquid and have a softer texture than steel-cut oats. Either kind can be used here, but note that steel-cut oats have a longer cooking time.

Chorizo, Egg, and Avocado Cups

SERVES 2 / PREP TIME: 10 minutes / COOK TIME: 20 minutes

Enjoy all the flavors of your favorite breakfast sandwich, inside an avocado! It's hard to think of a more palate-pleasing combo than sausage, egg, and cheese, unless, of course, you add avocado to the mix. Save the extra avocado you scoop out for toast. (Check out page 28 for some of my favorite breakfast-worthy combos.)

8 ounces chorizo sausage

2 large avocados, halved and pitted

4 medium eggs

Garlic salt

Freshly ground black pepper

½ cup shredded cheddar cheese

Hot sauce, for serving (optional)

Sour cream, for serving (optional)

1. Preheat the oven to 425°F.

2. Cut the chorizo in half, remove the casing, and break the sausage into chunks. In a large pan over medium heat, fry the chorizo chunks until cooked through but not crispy, about 8 minutes.

3. Use a spoon to carve out enough avocado from the center of each of the 4 halves to create shallow wells. You should still have some avocado flesh on the bottom and sides, but enough room for your fillings.

4. Place one quarter of the chorizo chunks into each well. Crack an egg into each, season with the garlic salt and pepper, and sprinkle the cheese on top.

5. Bake for 12 to 15 minutes, until the eggs are cooked through and set. Remove from the oven and cool for 5 minutes. Drizzle with the hot sauce and/or sour cream, if using, before serving.

I love using authentic Mexican hot sauce like Valentina with this recipe. It's the perfect combination of smoky chile flavor and a little bit of heat.

 Make a batch of your own garlic salt and keep it on hand for a salty, savory touch. Mix together a 3:1 ratio of salt to garlic powder and store.

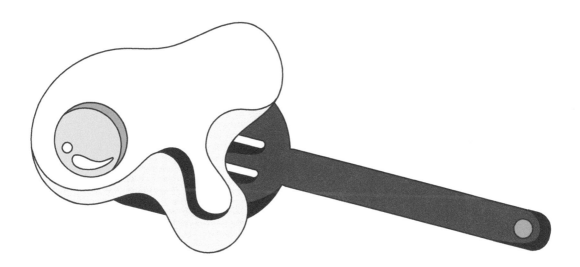

VEGETARIAN, GLUTEN-FREE, NUT-FREE

Squash, Red Pepper, and Feta Frittavo

SERVES 4 to 6 / PREP TIME: 15 minutes / COOK TIME: 30 minutes, plus 5 minutes to cool

I like to think of frittatas as pies you can eat first thing in the morning. This recipe uses squash and bell peppers, but feel free to throw in whatever greens or veggies may be lurking in the back of your produce drawer. While this recipe is very versatile and super easy, it also looks pretty enough to impress even the most discerning guests.

2 tablespoons olive oil

1 medium zucchini, chopped

½ cup diced red onion

1 red bell pepper, seeded and chopped

2 large avocados, pitted and peeled

8 large eggs

Sea salt

Freshly ground black pepper

1 cup crumbled feta cheese

½ cup diced cherry tomatoes

1. Preheat the oven to 350°F.

2. In a large (10-inch) cast-iron skillet over medium-high heat, heat the oil. Add the zucchini, onion, and bell pepper. Sauté, stirring occasionally, for 3 to 5 minutes.

3. In a medium bowl, mash one avocado with a fork until smooth. Slice the remaining avocado lengthwise and set aside.

4. In a large bowl, whisk the eggs, then add the mashed avocado and whisk until combined, or add the ingredients to a blender and pulse until smooth. Season with salt and pepper. Pour the egg mixture over the vegetables in the pan, sprinkle with the feta and tomatoes, and stir well.

5. Bake on the middle rack of the oven for 20 to 25 minutes or until the eggs are set in the middle. Remove from oven and let cool for 5 minutes.

6. Top with sliced avocado, and season with more salt and pepper. Cut and serve.

 No cast-iron pan? No worries! You can make this dish in a greased 9-inch cake pan. Just sauté your veggies in a skillet until they begin to soften, transfer them to the dish, and bake, uncovered, for 20 to 25 minutes, or until the eggs have set.

Very Verde Shakshuka

SERVES: 4 to 6 / PREP TIME: 20 minutes / COOK TIME: 20 minutes

This spicy twist on a centuries-old Mediterranean egg dish is one of my favorite brunch go-tos. It's easy to make and a surefire crowd-pleaser. The traditional version is made with a red sauce, but here we swap tomatoes for tomatillos, which give a bright green dish with a kick. Grab a crusty piece of bread or some pita so you can scoop up every bite of spicy, yolky goodness. Not a huge fan of heat? Just de-rib and seed the jalapeños before slicing for a milder take, or omit them altogether.

2 tablespoons olive oil

1 red onion, diced

1 green bell pepper, seeded and diced

2 garlic cloves, minced

2 jalapeño peppers, sliced, divided (optional)

½ teaspoon ground cumin

Sea salt

1 cup Aji Verde Sauce (page 94) or store-bought salsa verde

1 cup fresh or frozen chopped kale

6 large eggs

CONTINUED >

1. Preheat the oven to 375°F.

2. In a large (10-inch) cast-iron skillet, heat the oil over medium-low heat. Add the onion, bell pepper, garlic, 1 jalapeño, cumin, and salt to taste. Sauté for 5 minutes or until the peppers and onions are soft. Pour in the aji verde sauce and add the kale. Bring the mixture to a gentle simmer.

3. Make 6 small indentations in the sauce with the back of a spoon and gently crack an egg into each hollow. Sprinkle with the cheese and season with salt and pepper.

4. Bake in the oven for 10 to 15 minutes, until the eggs are cooked to your liking. (I like my eggs runny, so 10 minutes is perfect.) Carefully remove the skillet from the oven and let it rest for 5 minutes before serving. Freshly ground black pepper

½ cup cotija or feta cheese

Freshly ground black pepper

½ cup fresh cilantro

1 medium avocado, pitted,
   peeled and thinly sliced

Sour cream, for topping

1 lime, cut into wedges,
   for serving

5. Top with the remaining jalapeño, cilantro, avocado, and dollops of sour cream, and serve with the lime wedges.

In 2017, over 3 million photos of avocado toast were uploaded to Instagram.

Fluffy Avocado-and-Raspberry Flapjacks

SERVES: 4 / PREP TIME: 15 minutes / COOK TIME: 30 minutes

These vegan pancakes are fluffy, flavorful, and fruit-filled! This recipe can be easily adapted to fit most dietary preferences: Make these pancakes gluten-free by swapping in gluten-free flour. If dairy isn't an issue, use whatever milk you prefer. These also work well with any berries you have on hand. The avocado gives them a creamy texture you won't be able to resist.

1 cup all-purpose flour

1 teaspoon baking powder

½ teaspoon salt

2 bananas

1 large avocado, pitted and peeled

1 teaspoon fresh lime juice

3 tablespoons maple syrup, plus more for topping

½ teaspoon vanilla extract

1 teaspoon grated lime zest

¾ cup plant-based milk

1 tablespoon coconut oil or olive oil

½ cup fresh raspberries, plus more for topping, if desired

1. In a large bowl, whisk together the flour, baking powder, and salt.

2. In a separate bowl, mash the bananas, avocado, and lime juice with a fork until smooth. Whisk in the maple syrup, vanilla, lime zest, and milk. Add the avocado mixture to the flour mixture and stir until combined to form a batter.

3. In a large skillet, heat the oil over medium-low heat. Once melted, scoop a small amount of batter (about ¼ cup) into the pan and spread gently into a round shape with the back of a spoon.

4. Top each flapjack with a few raspberries. Cook 3 to 4 minutes per side until golden brown. Repeat with remaining batter (greasing the pan between batches, if needed).

5. To serve, top with more berries and maple syrup, if desired.

 For a deeper green color and a superfood boost, add some matcha powder to the batter.

Any leftover batter can last in an airtight container in the fridge for up to 1 day, so you can have these flapjacks all weekend long.

Chocolatey Sunflower Seed and Avocado Muffins

MAKES: 12 muffins / **PREP TIME:** 10 minutes / **COOK TIME:** 20 minutes

These muffins are so moist and delicious you can serve them for dessert, too. Rich, fudgy, and super easy to make, you would never guess that they don't have any dairy, gluten, oil, or refined sugar.

Nonstick cooking spray, for greasing

2¼ cups unsalted sunflower seeds, divided

1 cup unsweetened applesauce

1 large avocado, pitted, peeled, and mashed

½ cup unsweetened cocoa powder

½ cup maple syrup

1 teaspoon vanilla extract

1 teaspoon baking soda

2 to 4 tablespoons dairy-free chocolate chips (optional)

1. Preheat the oven to 350°F.
2. Spray a standard 12-cup muffin pan with nonstick cooking spray, or line with baking cups. Set aside.
3. In a blender, put 2 cups of the sunflower seeds, the applesauce, avocado, cocoa powder, maple syrup, vanilla, and baking soda, and blend until very smooth, about 1 minute.
4. Divide the mixture evenly among the muffin cups and top with the remaining sunflower seeds and chocolate chips, if using.
5. Bake for 20 minutes. The muffins are done when they're lightly browned and a toothpick inserted into the center comes out clean. Allow the muffins to cool completely before removing them from the pan.

If you'd like to prep these in advance, follow steps 1 through 4. Then pop the pan into the freezer until the batter is solid. Once frozen, remove your muffins to a freezer-safe resealable bag for later use. To bake, let thaw and bake as directed.

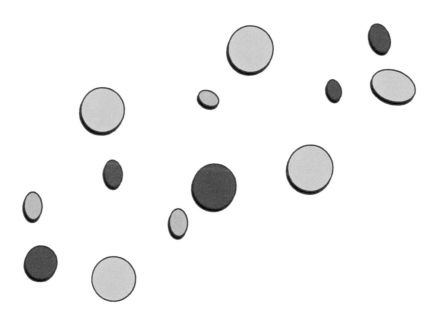

Avocado Toast: Breakfast Edition

The internet is full of toast-spiration, but here are some of my favorite twists, breakfast-style.

Bagel-Style Benedict
Your morning meal just got a major upgrade with this tasty version of the classic brunch bagel—with a Benedict twist.

 An English muffin with mashed avocado topped with sliced salmon lox, red onion, fresh dill, everything bagel seasoning, and Avocado Hollandaise (page 104).

Steak and Egg Texas Toast
Everything is bigger in Texas, including these bold breakfast flavors. It's a great way to use any leftover steak from the Avo-Cobb-o Steak Salad (page 54).

 Thick-sliced garlic bread topped with avocado mash, sliced steak, an over-easy egg, and hot sauce.

Mango and Avocado Tostada
Mango and avocado come together on a crunchy tortilla for a tropical take on a breakfast taco.

 A baked tortilla spread with mashed avocado, topped with diced mango, a squeeze of lime juice, and a dash of cayenne pepper.

Chapter 3

APPS, SNACKS & SIDES

Chili and Lime Avo Crisps

SERVES: 4 to 6 / PREP TIME: 10 minutes / COOK TIME: 20 minutes

If you thought avocados couldn't get any more versatile, here's another way to slice them: into crispy, crunchy, spicy chips that are so savory and satisfying, it's almost shocking to think they come from fruit! Dusted in a light coat of chili powder and paprika, they are perfect for snacking or dipped in Avocado Blanco Dip (page 95). Don't hesitate to play around with flavors in these chips. Ditch the Parmesan for a vegetarian take, or go deliciously simple with just sea salt and lime juice.

1 large avocado, pitted
    and peeled
½ cup freshly grated
    Parmesan cheese
1 teaspoon grated lime zest
1 teaspoon fresh lime juice
½ teaspoon garlic powder
½ teaspoon onion powder
½ teaspoon red pepper flakes
Sea salt
Freshly ground black pepper
1½ teaspoons chili powder
½ teaspoon paprika

1. Preheat the oven to 325°F. Line a baking sheet with parchment paper.

2. In a large bowl, mash the avocado with a fork until smooth. Mix in the cheese, lime zest and juice, garlic powder, onion powder, and red pepper flakes. Season with salt and pepper.

3. Using a teaspoon, scoop small balls of the avocado mixture and place them on the baking sheet, leaving 1 inch between each. Using the back of the spoon, flatten each ball into a disk shape, so that it is thin like a cracker.

4. Bake for about 20 minutes, or until crisp and golden, then let cool completely. Dust with the chili powder, paprika, and more salt to taste.

DAIRY-FREE, GLUTEN-FREE

Tangy Shrimp-and-Avocado Ceviche

SERVES: 6 to 8 / PREP TIME: 10 minutes, plus 50 minutes to marinate / COOK TIME: 5 minutes

This cool, light, and refreshing Latin American–inspired favorite offers a flavor explosion for your taste buds. This ceviche, made with just a few simple ingredients like zesty lime, buttery avocado, and juicy tomatoes, makes a crowd-pleasing appetizer, lunch, or even a light dinner when served on top of a salad or in a taco shell or a wrap.

1 pound raw jumbo shrimp, peeled and deveined

1 cup fresh lime juice (from 6 to 8 limes)

½ cup fresh orange juice

2 tablespoons olive oil

Sea salt

Freshly ground black pepper

1 large tomato

1 medium red onion

1 medium cucumber

1 jalapeño

1 medium avocado, pitted, peeled, and diced

½ cup fresh cilantro, chopped

1 lime, cut into wedges, for serving

1. Bring a large pot of water to a boil. Add the shrimp and boil for 3 minutes, or until pink. Drain the shrimp into a colander. When cool enough to handle, dice and set aside.

2. In a large bowl, combine the lime juice, orange juice, oil, and shrimp. Season with salt and pepper. Stir to combine. Let the mixture marinate in the refrigerator for 30 minutes.

3. Meanwhile, finely dice the tomato, onion, cucumber, and jalapeño, and set aside until the shrimp is done marinating. If you're not a fan of heat, seed and de-rib the jalapeño before dicing.

4. After 30 minutes, add the vegetables to the bowl with the shrimp. Return to the refrigerator for another 20 minutes. Just before serving, stir in the avocado and cilantro. Serve with lime wedges.

Avo Fries with Lime Mayo

SERVES: 2 (makes about 15 fries) / PREP TIME: 10 minutes / COOK TIME: 20 minutes

Grab your dipping sauce—there's a new fry in town. Avocado fries are the crispy, crunchy, rich, and creamy fry you never knew you wanted. They are a perfect way to use an overripe avocado and give a healthier spin to a fast-food fave. Enjoy these with the spicy Lime Mayo below or the Avocado Blanco Dip on page 95, or give plain old ketchup something to talk about.

For the avo fries

Olive oil, for greasing
1 teaspoon garlic salt
1 teaspoon cayenne pepper
½ cup all-purpose flour
Freshly ground black pepper
2 large eggs
1½ cups bread crumbs
3 medium avocados, pitted,
    peeled, and sliced into
    1-inch wedges

For the lime mayo

1 tablespoon fresh lime juice
1 cup mayonnaise
1 teaspoon garlic salt
1 teaspoon cayenne pepper

1. Preheat the oven to 425°F. Grease a large baking sheet with oil and set it aside.

2. Set up a dredging station for the fries: In a medium bowl, combine the garlic salt, cayenne pepper, and flour. Season with black pepper. In a small bowl, beat the eggs. In another medium bowl, put the bread crumbs.

3. Dip each avocado slice in the flour mixture, then the eggs, and then bread crumbs. Toss gently to ensure that the bread crumbs stick. Place the coated avocado slices on the prepared baking sheet. Bake for 15 to 20 minutes, or until golden.

4. While the avocado fries bake, make the lime mayo. In a small bowl, put the lime juice and mayonnaise. Add the garlic salt and cayenne pepper and mix until well combined. Refrigerate until needed.

5. Once the fries are done, let them cool completely before serving with the lime mayo.

For less heat, leave out the cayenne pepper and swap in your favorite herb, like dried rosemary or oregano, in either or both recipes.

If you don't have garlic salt, see the tip on page 19 for how incredibly easy it is to make your own or substitute 3/4 teaspoon sea salt.

Heavenly Deviled Eggs

MAKES: 16 deviled eggs / PREP TIME: 15 minutes / COOK TIME: 8 minutes

I had to indulge in some wordplay, because contrary to their traditional name, these deviled eggs are sent from heaven. This appetizer classic gets a much-deserved update, along with a burst of color, by adding avocado and tarragon. I've found that the key to the creamiest filling is getting the perfect jammy eggs with about a 6-minute boil—the yolkier, the creamier. To make these eggs vegetarian, just omit the Parmesan.

8 eggs

1 medium avocado, pitted, peeled, and mashed

3 tablespoons mayonnaise

2 tablespoons yellow mustard

¼ teaspoon garlic powder

⅛ teaspoon cayenne pepper

2 teaspoons fresh lime juice

Sea salt

Freshly ground black pepper

2 tablespoons chopped fresh tarragon, for garnish

Paprika, for garnish

¼ cup grated Parmesan cheese, for garnish (optional)

1. In a large saucepan, bring 2 inches of water to a boil. Add the eggs in a single layer in the bottom of the pot, working in batches if necessary. Cover the pot and boil for 6 minutes. Remove the eggs to a colander, run them under cool water, then peel.

2. Slice the eggs in half lengthwise and scoop the yolks into a large bowl. Place the egg whites cut-side up on a platter and refrigerate until ready to fill.

3. In the bowl with the egg yolks, add the avocado, mayonnaise, mustard, garlic powder, cayenne pepper, and lime juice. Season with salt and pepper and mix with a fork or whisk until creamy.

4. Remove the egg whites from the refrigerator and, using a teaspoon, evenly divide the filling among the egg whites, and sprinkle with tarragon, paprika, and Parmesan, if using. Refrigerate until ready to serve.

 Prep the egg whites and filling up to 3 days in advance, and refrigerate each separately in tightly sealed containers until ready to assemble and serve.

 Give your eggs the star treatment by piping the egg yolk mixture into the egg whites using a piping bag fitted with a star tip (or cut off the corner of a plastic sandwich bag).

GLUTEN-FREE, VEGETARIAN

Avocado-Stuffed Pepper Jack Jalapeños

MAKES: 20 poppers / PREP TIME: 10 Minutes / COOK TIME: 20 minutes, plus 10 minutes to cool

Jalapeños take center stage in this zesty, cheesy, spicy snack, stuffed with melty pepper Jack cheese and creamy avocado. It's a delicious combination that will satisfy the most discerning snack connoisseur. If you like the idea but can't stand the heat, use mini bell peppers in place of jalapeños and cut down the amount of red pepper flakes. The flavor still bursts, but your mouth won't!

10 jalapeño peppers

1 (8-ounce) package cream cheese, softened

1 large avocado, pitted and peeled

Juice of 1 lime

1 teaspoon red pepper flakes

Sea salt

Freshly ground black pepper

8 ounces shredded pepper Jack cheese

1. Preheat the oven to 425°F. Line a baking sheet with aluminum foil and set aside.

2. Slice the jalapeños in half lengthwise and use a spoon to scoop out and discard the seeds. Place the jalapeño halves on the baking sheet.

3. In a large bowl, combine the cream cheese, avocado, lime juice, red pepper flakes, and salt and pepper to taste until smooth. Spoon the filling into the prepared jalapeño halves. Sprinkle each with the pepper Jack cheese.

4. Bake for 20 minutes or until the cheese has melted. If you want a crispy cheese topping, put the baking sheet under the broiler for 1 minute, watching carefully to prevent burning.

5. Remove from the oven and allow to cool for 5 to 10 minutes before serving. Serve warm.

Make sure to wear gloves or coat your hands in olive oil while you handle these peppers, and whatever you do, don't touch your eyes.

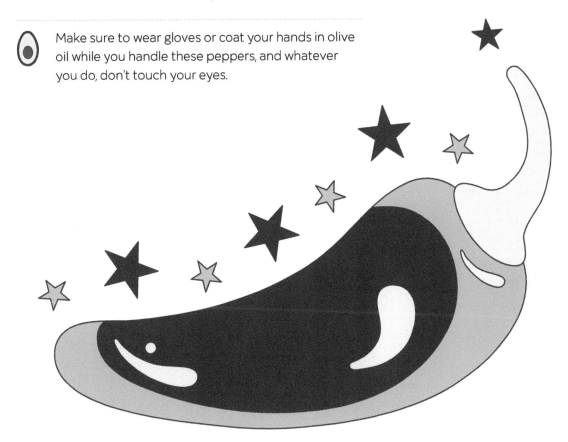

Avocado-Stuffed Plantain Scoops

MAKES: 12 bites / PREP TIME: 20 minutes / COOK TIME: 15 minutes

These plantain scoops filled with creamy avocado will sweep you and your guests away to the islands with every bite. Plantains are part of the banana family but are starchier and less sweet, making them perfect for savory appetizers like these. Even better, these banana doppelgängers are a rich source of fiber, vitamins A and C, and more.

Olive oil, for greasing

4 ripe plantains, peeled

Sea salt

Freshly ground black pepper

2 avocados, halved and pitted

Juice of 1 lime

1 medium tomato, diced

1 medium onion, diced

Chopped fresh cilantro,
   for garnish

1. Preheat the oven to 425°F. Grease a standard 12-cup muffin pan with oil.

2. In a large bowl, mash the plantains well, then scoop about 1 tablespoon into each muffin cup. Using the back of a spoon or your fingers, press the plantains into the cavities to form a cup. Coat each cup with more oil and season with salt and pepper. Place the muffin pan in the oven and bake for 10 to 15 minutes, until the plantains are crispy. Remove from the oven and set aside to cool.

3. While the plantains are in the oven, scoop the avocado flesh into a large bowl. Add the lime juice and season with more salt and pepper. Mash together until well combined. Stir in the tomato and onion.

4. Remove the plantain cups from the muffin pan and set on a plate. Divide the avocado mixture evenly among the plantain cups, and top each with cilantro. Serve immediately.

 Try these bites with different fillings like refried beans, hummus, or even ground beef.

Loaded Sweet Potato Nachos

SERVES: 4 to 6 / PREP TIME: 15 minutes / COOK TIME: 25 minutes

You know the old saying, "Nothing says lovin' like nachos from the oven," right? Well, maybe that's just me, but I think this dish is the definition of devotion! Buried under the piles of avocado, black beans, fresh jalapeño slices, red onion, and of course, *cheese* is a healthy secret of sliced sweet potatoes instead of tortilla chips.

3 large sweet potatoes, peeled and sliced into ¼-inch-thick rounds

2 tablespoons olive oil

1 teaspoon garlic powder

1 teaspoon chili powder

Sea salt

Freshly ground black pepper

1 cup shredded cheddar cheese

1 (15-ounce) can black beans, drained and rinsed

1 cup diced red onion

2 jalapeños, sliced

2 medium avocados, pitted, peeled, and diced

CONTINUED >

1. Preheat the oven to 425°F and line a large baking sheet with foil.

2. In a large bowl, combine the sweet potato slices and oil and toss to coat. Add the garlic and chili powders and season with salt and pepper. Toss again to evenly distribute the spices.

3. Arrange the sweet potato rounds on the baking pan in a single layer. Bake for about 20 minutes.

4. Remove the pan from the oven and flip the sweet potatoes. Sprinkle with about half of the cheese, then top with the beans, onion, jalapeños, avocado, and the remaining cheese.

5. Return to the oven and bake for about 10 minutes, or until the cheese melts and the sweet potatoes begin to brown around the edges. You can also skip baking again and set the pan under the broiler for 3 to 5 minutes.

Aji Verde Sauce (page 94), Avocado Blanco Dip (page 95), or sour cream, for serving

¼ cup fresh cilantro, for topping

1 lime, cut into wedges, for serving

Hot sauce, for serving (optional)

6. Remove the nachos from the oven and drizzle with your sauce of choice. Sprinkle the cilantro on top and serve with the lime wedges and hot sauce, if using.

 Authentic Mexican hot sauce, like Valentina brand, with its smoky, less spicy flavor, is perfect on this recipe, but a verde hot sauce would be a nice complement, too.

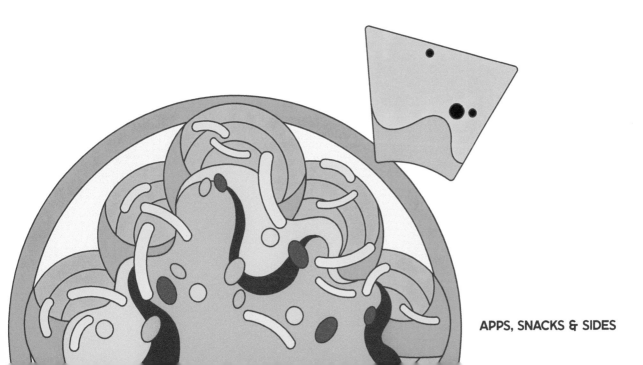

Sweet Avocado Spring Rolls with Lemon-Tahini Dipping Sauce

MAKES: 6 rolls / PREP TIME: 20 minutes

You'll feel you're taking a bite out of summertime with these bright, fresh spring rolls. Play around with the ingredients and mix and match your favorites. Spring roll wrappers are made of rice, so they're gluten-free. Find them in the international aisle of large grocery stores or in most Asian food stores. You can also try different wraps, like collard green leaves, seaweed, or tapioca sheets. Any way you roll it, these Asian-inspired delicacies make fantastic finger food or a mouth-watering meal.

For the spring rolls

6 spring roll wrappers

¼ cup fresh mint leaves

4 large iceberg lettuce leaves, cut in half

1 small carrot, julienned

1 small cucumber, julienned

½ cup strawberries, thinly sliced

1 mango, peeled, pitted, sliced

1 medium avocado, pitted, peeled, and sliced lengthwise

CONTINUED >

To make the spring rolls

1. In a 9-by-13-inch baking dish filled with 1 inch of warm water, soak a spring roll wrapper for 10 seconds and then transfer to a clean, damp kitchen towel.

2. Lay the wrapper flat and start by placing a few mint leaves and a piece of the lettuce on each. Then add 2 to 3 pieces each of carrot, cucumber, strawberry, mango, avocado, rice noodles, basil, and jalapeño, and sprinkle with sesame seeds. Placing the smaller veggies in a lettuce "cup" helps keep them in place when you roll.

4 ounces rice noodles, cooked
according to package
instructions

¼ cup fresh basil leaves

1 jalapeño, seeded and
julienned

1 teaspoon sesame seeds

**For the lemon-tahini
dipping sauce**

Juice of 1 lemon

2 cups tahini

1 cup honey

1 teaspoon grated
fresh ginger

Sea salt

Freshly ground
black pepper

3. Fold the bottom of the wrapper over the filling, then fold each of the sides into the center and roll upward, tucking the wrapper as you go to form a roll. Repeat the process with the remaining spring roll wrappers and ingredients.

To make the lemon-tahini dipping sauce

4. In a small bowl, whisk together the lemon juice, tahini, honey, and ginger. Taste and season with salt and pepper.

 Tahini is a creamy butter made from sesame seeds. If you can't find it, peanut butter is a perfect substitution.

 Any leftover dipping sauce can be stored in an airtight container and refrigerated for up to a week. It makes a great salad dressing!

Baked Brie with Sliced Avocado and Pomegranate Seeds

SERVES: 4 to 6 / PREP TIME: 5 minutes / COOK TIME: 10 minutes

Rich, buttery Brie, topped with sweet, tangy pomegranate seeds and creamy avocado, drizzled with honey, and sprinkled with sunflower seeds—*Ooh la la!* You've got a showstopping appetizer that looks as elegant as it tastes. The best part? This magical recipe goes from zero to party in just 15 minutes.

1 (13-ounce) wheel
  Brie cheese
1 medium avocado, pitted,
  peeled, and sliced
1 cup pomegranate seeds
2 tablespoons unsalted
  sunflower seeds
3 to 4 fresh rosemary sprigs,
  for garnish
Honey, for drizzling
1 teaspoon olive oil or
  avocado oil, for drizzling
Sea salt
Crackers or toasted bread,
  for serving

1. Preheat the oven to 350°F. Line a baking sheet with parchment paper.

2. Place the wheel of Brie on the baking sheet. Bake for 10 minutes, or until the cheese is soft and begins to melt out of the rind.

3. Remove it from the oven and transfer to a serving platter. Top it with the avocado slices, pomegranate seeds, sunflower seeds, and rosemary, and drizzle with the honey and oil. Sprinkle with salt, and serve with crackers or toasted bread.

 Sunflower seeds provide a great nut-free crunch to this recipe, but feel free to swap them for chopped pistachios or crushed walnuts to change the flavor a bit.

GLUTEN-FREE, 30 MINUTES OR LESS, VEGETARIAN

California Caprese Skewers

MAKES: 12 (6-inch) skewers / PREP TIME: 10 minutes

The classic caprese salad has been transformed into a fresh and fabulous appetizer to go! Each skewer is stacked with avocado, cherry tomatoes, mozzarella, fresh basil, and a sweet balsamic drizzle. Perfect for parties, they may be quick and easy to make, but they are almost impossible to stop eating. For an eco-friendly option, invest in reusable metal skewers (since you'll want to make these all summer long).

1 pint cherry tomatoes

2 large avocados, pitted, peeled, and diced

1 bunch fresh basil

1 (4-ounce) ball fresh mozzarella, cut into 1-inch cubes

Balsamic vinegar, for drizzling

Sea salt

Freshly ground black pepper

1. On each skewer, spear a tomato and one cube of avocado. Fold a basil leaf in half, then add that to the skewer, followed by a mozzarella cube. Keep going in that order (tomato, avocado, basil, mozzarella) until the skewer is full. (Don't forget to leave enough room to hold it!) Place each finished skewer on a platter, and repeat the process until all skewers and ingredients have been used.

2. To serve, drizzle the skewers with the balsamic vinegar and sprinkle with salt and pepper to taste.

 Load these up with more veggies like red onion or cucumbers. No skewers? Throw all the ingredients in a bowl to make a great salad.

Avocado Toast: Apps, Snacks & Sides Edition

Perfectly portable for a side dish or appetizer, try out these *appetizing* bites.

Cucumber-Avocado Bites

These are summer in a slider, crispy and refreshing with a cooling minty touch.

 Sliced cucumbers with a dollop of avocado mash, topped with a cube of pineapple and a fresh mint leaf.

Sweet-and-Savory Roasted Carrot and Thyme Toast

Carrot cake meets avocado toast in this combination that is almost too good to be good for you.

 A slice of toasted multigrain bread covered in creamy goat cheese, topped with roasted carrots, sliced avocado, sea salt, and thyme, and drizzled with honey.

Chapter 4

SALADS, SOUPS & SANDWICHES

DAIRY-FREE, 30 MINUTES OR LESS, VEGETARIAN

Creamy Avocado Coleslaw

SERVES: 4 to 6 / PREP TIME: 15 minutes

It doesn't have to be hot outside to enjoy this summery twist on a Dutch-turned-American favorite. Tangy lemon juice and creamy avocado tossed with a slightly sweet dressing give a refreshing yet delicate flavor to the crispy, crunchy cabbage.

3 cups shredded
   green cabbage
3 cups shredded
   red cabbage
1½ cups finely diced
   sweet onion
2 cups shredded carrot
2 medium avocados, pitted
   and peeled
¼ cup fresh lemon juice
   (from 1 to 2 lemons)
1 tablespoon honey
¼ cup red wine vinegar
Sea salt
Freshly ground black pepper

1. In a large bowl, combine the green and red cabbage, onion, and carrot.

2. In a separate bowl, mash the avocados and stir in the lemon juice, honey, vinegar, and salt and pepper to taste, and mix until smooth.

3. Stir the avocado mixture into the cabbage mixture. Season with more salt and pepper, if desired. Serve chilled.

DAIRY-FREE, 30 MINUTES OR LESS, VEGETARIAN

Southwestern Succotash

SERVES: 6 to 8 / PREP TIME: 15 minutes, plus at least 15 minutes to chill

This Southwestern-inspired sort-of-salad suffers from none of the humdrum of its peers. Loaded with corn, tomato, black beans and of course, avocado, it's a bowl full of fresh and fabulous flavor. Eat it by the spoonful, ladle a little on your tacos or burger, or scoop it up with Chili and Lime Avo Crisps (page 32).

2 (15-ounce) cans black beans, drained and rinsed

1 (15-ounce) can cooked corn, drained and rinsed

2 red bell peppers, seeded and diced

1 large tomato, diced

¼ cup minced red onion

1 jalapeño, seeded and diced

¼ cup olive oil

Juice of 1 lime

2 teaspoons honey

¼ teaspoon chili powder

1 teaspoon ground cumin

3 garlic cloves, minced

½ cup chopped fresh cilantro, plus more for garnish

Sea salt

Freshly ground black pepper

2 medium avocados, pitted, peeled, and diced

1. In a large bowl, combine the black beans, corn, bell peppers, tomato, onion, and jalapeño.

2. In a separate bowl, whisk together the oil, lime juice, honey, chili powder, cumin, garlic, cilantro, and salt and pepper to taste. Pour this dressing over the bean-and-corn mixture, and toss gently to coat.

3. Cover and chill for at least 15 minutes or overnight. Right before serving, add the avocados and mix gently. Garnish with more chopped cilantro and serve cold or at room temperature.

30 MINUTES OR LESS, GLUTEN-FREE

Avo-Cobb-o Steak Salad with Creamy Blue Cheese Dressing

SERVES 4 / PREP TIME: 20 minutes / COOK TIME: 10 minutes

Did someone order a steak . . . salad? This loaded avocado Cobb salad stands as a meal all on its own. Based on the famed favorite that originated in Hollywood, this avocado-boosted version will please even the hungriest meat eaters. Don't be fooled by the name I made up—this salad is serious business.

For the dressing

2 medium avocados, pitted
    and peeled
2 cups crumbled blue cheese
¼ cup fresh lemon juice
    (from 1 to 2 lemons)
½ cup water
Sea salt
Freshly ground black pepper

For the salad

1 to 1½ pounds flank steak
Sea salt
Freshly ground black pepper
1 tablespoon olive oil
8 cups chopped
    romaine lettuce

To make the dressing

1. In a blender, combine the avocados, blue cheese, lemon juice, and water. Blend until smooth and creamy, 30 to 40 seconds. Add more water if needed to reach a pourable consistency. Season with salt and pepper. Refrigerate until ready to use.

To make the salad

2. Season the steak with salt and pepper. In a nonstick skillet over medium heat, heat the oil. Sear the steak for 3 to 4 minutes per side for medium-rare. It should reach an internal temperature of 145°F. Remove from the pan and let it rest on a cutting board for 5 minutes before chopping. Set aside.

3. In a large bowl, place the lettuce, diced avocado, tomatoes, onion, eggs, blue cheese, bacon, and steak. Toss to combine. Pour dressing on top and toss to coat.

2 medium avocados, pitted,
   peeled, and diced
1 cup cherry
   tomatoes, chopped
½ cup chopped red onion
4 hard-boiled eggs, chopped
½ cup crumbled blue cheese
½ cup crumbled
   cooked bacon

 I chose flank steak here, but any steak will do. Or give it a try with chicken or salmon.

 This dressing also makes a great dip for Chili and Lime Avo Crisps (page 32) or, Avocado-Stuffed Pepper Jack Jalapeños (page 38), or your favorite chicken wings.

DAIRY-FREE, GLUTEN-FREE

Kickin' Avocado Chicken Salad

SERVES: 6 / PREP TIME: 10 minutes, plus 2 hours to marinate / COOK TIME: 20 minutes

Creamy chunks of avocado paired with tender pieces of chicken give a classic new life. Pile this salad on a bed of lettuce, spread it between two pieces of your favorite bread, or just enjoy it by the forkful like me. Too spicy for you? This chicken salad can host all sorts of flavors. Sub in fresh grapes for the jalapeños and balsamic vinaigrette for the hot sauce. You can even add some walnuts for crunch and texture.

1 pound boneless, skinless chicken breasts

1 tablespoon ground cumin

Sea salt

Freshly ground black pepper

2 tablespoons fresh lime juice, divided

2 tablespoons avocado oil or olive oil, divided

½ cup hot sauce

2 medium avocados, pitted and peeled

½ cup diced red onion

½ cup diced jalapeños

¼ cup chopped fresh cilantro

2 teaspoons paprika

1. In a large bowl, place the chicken and season with the cumin, salt and pepper to taste, 1 tablespoon of lime juice, 1 tablespoon of oil, and hot sauce. Mix well, cover, and refrigerate for 2 hours, or overnight at most.

2. Preheat the oven to 375°F. Transfer the marinated chicken to a baking dish, drizzle with the remaining 1 tablespoon of oil, and bake for 20 minutes or until cooked through and no longer pink. Remove the chicken from the oven and allow it to rest in the pan. Once cool, shred the chicken with two forks (see tip below) and set aside.

3. In another large bowl, combine the avocados, onion, jalapeño, cilantro, and remaining 1 tablespoon of lime juice, and mix until smooth. Add the chicken and toss until evenly coated. Sprinkle with the paprika before serving.

To shred the chicken without using your hands, use two forks. Hold one fork in each hand and use them to pull the meat apart.

Store leftovers in an airtight container in the fridge for up to 4 days. I think it tastes even better on day 2 or 3 once the flavors have had a chance to really develop.

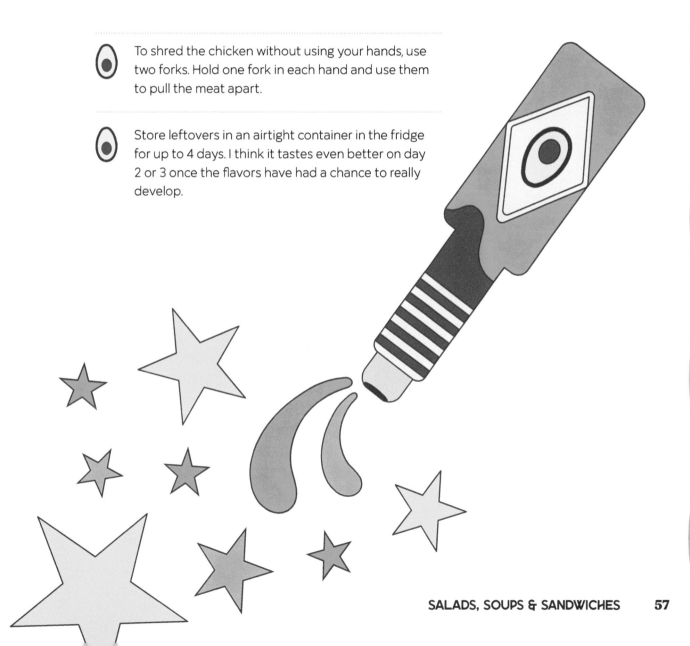

DAIRY-FREE, GLUTEN-FREE, VEGETARIAN

Roasted Yellow Pepper and Avocado Bisque

SERVES: 4 to 6 / PREP TIME: 10 minutes / COOK TIME: 30 minutes

While a rich, velvety bowl of this creamy bisque will nourish you in the cooler weather, it's just as delicious chilled—so eat it year-round! You can store leftovers in an airtight container in the refrigerator for a week or freeze it for up to 4 months. If you and dairy get along, top each bowl with a healthy dollop of Greek yogurt before serving.

4 large yellow bell peppers, seeded and halved

5 garlic cloves

1 large yellow onion, chopped

2 tablespoons olive oil

1 (15-ounce) can diced tomatoes

1 cup coconut milk

2 cups vegetable broth

2 teaspoons ground cumin

1 teaspoon smoked paprika

1 teaspoon cayenne pepper

1 teaspoon dried basil

Sea salt

Freshly ground black pepper

2 medium avocados, pitted and peeled

1. Line a baking sheet with foil and arrange the bell peppers on it, cut-side down. Add the garlic and onion, and drizzle everything with the oil. Place the baking sheet on the middle rack of the oven and broil on low until peppers are blackened across the top, about 4 to 5 minutes.

2. In a large pot, place the tomatoes, coconut milk, broth, cumin, paprika, cayenne pepper, basil, and salt and pepper to taste. Stir together and let simmer for 8 to 10 minutes. Remove from heat and let cool slightly.

3. In a blender, combine the cooled tomato mixture, roasted vegetables, and avocado. Working in batches if necessary, blend the ingredients until smooth, using caution as the liquid might be hot. You can also add the roasted vegetables to the pot and blend with an immersion blender.

4. Return the soup to the pot and simmer for 10 more minutes. To serve, divide the soup into individual bowls and top with more freshly ground black pepper.

 You can also roast the vegetables in step 1. Place them on a foil-lined baking sheet and bake at 400°F for 20 minutes, flip the peppers, and bake for 20 minutes more. Check on your onions and garlic at the halfway point, as they might be done roasting before the peppers.

Pesto, Parmesan, and Avocado Toasties

SERVES: 2 / PREP TIME: 5 minutes / COOK TIME: 8 minutes

This variation on grilled cheese has earned its place in the Avo Hall of Fame. Picture this: nutty multigrain bread, toasted to perfection, stacked with a thick slice of tomato, slathered in a homemade Creamy Avocado Pesto (page 96), and oozing sharp Parmesan cheese in every bite. Make it even more magical by adding some slices of prosciutto or sliced jalapeño to the melty mix.

2 medium avocados, pitted, peeled, and mashed

¼ cup Creamy Avocado Pesto (page 96) or store-bought pesto

1 cup shredded Parmesan cheese, divided

1 tablespoon olive oil, for greasing

4 slices multigrain bread

1 medium beefsteak tomato, sliced

½ small white onion, thinly sliced

Sea salt

Freshly ground black pepper

1 tablespoon mayonnaise, divided

1. In a large bowl, mix together the avocados, pesto, and ½ cup of Parmesan cheese, and set aside.

2. Grease a nonstick pan with the oil. Make 2 toasties by laying out 4 slices of bread. Spread the pesto over all 4 slices. To 2 of the slices, add 2 slices of tomato and 2 slices of onion, sprinkle with the remaining cheese, and season with salt and pepper to taste. Top with the remaining 2 slices of bread. Spread the outside of these 2 pieces of bread with a thin layer of mayonnaise and place the toasties in the pan.

3. Cook over medium heat until lightly browned; flip and continue cooking until the cheese is melted, approximately 2 minutes per side.

Refreshing Cilantro, Lime, and Avocado Soup

SERVES: 4 / PREP TIME: 20 minutes, plus 2 hours to chill

Who says gazpacho gets to have all the fun? Sorry, tomatoes, but this cool, creamy soup is here to give you a run for your money. Packed with avocado, lime juice, and cilantro, this Peruvian-inspired dish is the perfect mix of flavors for a hot summer day. Add in some roasted chicken or potatoes to make a heartier meal.

6 medium avocados, pitted
  and peeled
4 cups vegetable broth
1 small white onion
Juice of 2 limes
½ cup fresh cilantro, chopped,
  plus more for garnish
Sea salt
Freshly ground black pepper
4 tablespoons sour cream, for
  serving (optional)
1 jalapeño, seeded and diced,
  for serving (optional)

1. In a blender, combine the avocados, broth, onion, lime juice, cilantro, and salt and pepper to taste. Process until smooth. Transfer to a large bowl, cover, and refrigerate for 2 hours.

2. To serve, divide soup among 4 bowls, top each with a dollop of sour cream and diced jalapeño, if using, and garnish with the remaining cilantro. This soup can be stored in an airtight container in the fridge for up to a week. Just give it a good stir before serving.

The "Godmother" Collard Green Heroine Wraps

SERVES: 4 to 6 / PREP TIME: 10 minutes / COOK TIME: 5 minutes

Create a new favorite, and fancier, foot-long with this collard-green-wrapped version of the Italian deli classic. It boasts all the typical fresh veggies and sliced meats and cheese of the traditional "Godfather" hero, but lifts it out of this world with the addition of sliced avocado and spicy hummus.

6 collard green leaves

¼ cup water

⅓ cup Italian seasoning

⅓ cup olive oil

⅓ cup red wine vinegar

2 tablespoons Jalapeño and
 Avocado Hummus (page 98),
 or store-bought hummus

6 turkey breast slices,
 cut in half

6 provolone cheese slices,
 cut in half

6 pepperoni slices, cut in half

1 medium tomato, thinly sliced

1 medium onion, thinly sliced

2 medium avocados, pitted,
 peeled, and sliced

CONTINUED >

1. Lay the collard green leaves on a flat surface and score down the stems so that each leaf flattens , but is not cut in half. In a large pan, heat the water over medium heat. Add the collard greens to the pan and steam for 1 to 2 minutes, until soft. Remove them from the pan and dry with paper towels.

2. In a small bowl, combine the Italian seasoning, oil, and vinegar. Whisk together with a fork and set aside.

3. Spread an even layer of hummus over each of the leaves. Layer each with 2 pieces of turkey, 2 pieces of provolone, 2 pieces of pepperoni, 2 slices of tomato, 2 slices of onion, and 2 slices of avocado. Top with slices of banana peppers, if using, olives, and romaine. Drizzle with the dressing and season with salt and pepper to taste.

¼ cup sliced banana
   peppers (optional)
¼ cup sliced black olives
2 cups shredded
   romaine lettuce
Sea salt
Freshly ground black pepper

4. Form a wrap by folding each side of the collard leaves inward and tucking in the bottom (like a burrito). Continue to roll into a neat and tight wrap. Secure with a toothpick or wrap in parchment paper, if needed.

 Collard wraps are easy to customize: Change up the fillings with a variety of meats, cheeses, and veggies. Or use your favorite sauce and make them your own.

Marinated Mushroom and Fried Avocado Fajita Salad

SERVES: 6 / PREP TIME: 15 minutes / COOK TIME: 15 minutes

Marinated mushrooms and crispy fried avocado make the perfect toppings for this five-star veggie fajita salad. The main attraction is the crunchy Avo Fries (page 34), but using regular sliced avocado works as well, too; either way, this salad will have everyone asking for the recipe, especially when you top it with some crushed tortilla chips for texture.

2 tablespoons olive oil

Juice of 1 lime

1 teaspoon ground cumin

1 teaspoon chipotle powder

½ teaspoon garlic powder

1 cup thinly sliced
   shiitake mushrooms

1 cup thinly sliced
   portabella mushrooms

1 yellow onion, thinly sliced

1 red bell pepper, thinly sliced

1 yellow bell pepper,
   thinly sliced

1 green bell pepper,
   thinly sliced

CONTINUED ›

1. In a medium bowl, whisk together the oil, lime juice, cumin, chipotle powder, and garlic powder. Add the mushrooms, onion, and bell peppers to the bowl and mix until evenly coated.

2. Heat a large skillet over medium heat. Cook the vegetables for 5 to 8 minutes, until tender. Remove the veggies from the skillet and set aside.

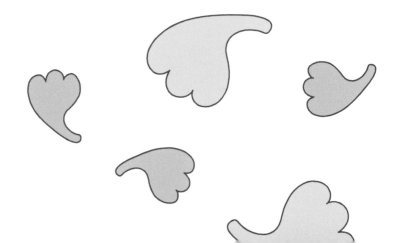

4 cups chopped
  romaine lettuce
2 large Avo Fries (page 34)
¼ cup fresh cilantro,
  for garnish
Salsa, for serving
Sour cream, for serving

3. Fill a large bowl with the lettuce and top with the mush-room mix, Avo Fries, cilantro, salsa, and sour cream.

 The possible toppings for this fajita salad are endless. Be creative and add some Southwestern Succotash (page 53), Avocado Blanco Dip (page 95), or LP's Spoon-Lickin' Roasted Garlic Guac (page 100).

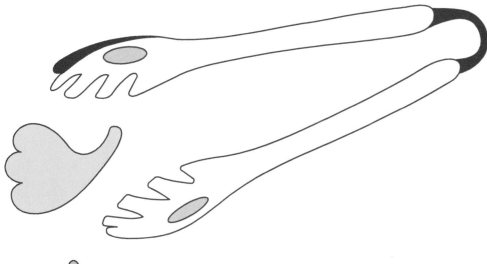

GLUTEN-FREE, VEGETARIAN

Summer-Ready Watermelon, Feta, and Avocado Salad

SERVES: 6 / PREP TIME: 10 minutes, plus 30 minutes to chill

You'll experience a burst of summer with each refreshing bite of this easy salad. Sweet, juicy watermelon, fresh avocado, cucumbers, feta, and mint create a dish just perfect for those warm-weather picnics, potlucks, and porch hangouts. The sweet-and-salty combination pairs perfectly with grilled chicken or fish.

2 cups diced fresh watermelon

1 medium avocado, pitted, peeled, and diced

1 small cucumber, diced

¼ tablespoon avocado oil or olive oil

½ cup diced fresh cilantro

Grated zest and juice of 1 lime

½ cup crumbled feta cheese

¼ cup fresh mint leaves

Sea salt

In a large bowl, combine watermelon, avocado, cucumber, oil, cilantro, lime zest and juice, feta, and mint, and gently toss. Season with salt. Refrigerate for 30 minutes, and serve chilled.

 Salty feta is perfect in this dish, but fresh mozzarella balls or crumbled goat cheese would be just as tasty.

Avocado Toast: Salads, Soups & Sandwiches Edition

Avocado toast is already a lunch staple, so give it a tasty protein boost with these ideas.

Balsamic Mushroom and Garlicky Avocado Sourdough
A hearty sourdough slice loaded with meaty mushrooms turns this typical toast into a full meal.

⭐ Sourdough toast covered in a garlic-avocado mash, topped with sautéed sliced portabella mushrooms, and drizzled with balsamic vinaigrette.

Sprouted Avocado Tuna Melt
This fresh open-faced take on the tuna melt will have you running to the toaster oven.

⭐ Toasted rye bread slathered with cream cheese mixed with mashed avocado and topped with flaky albacore tuna and sprouts.

Chapter 5

Sesame Shrimp-and-Avocado Lettuce Wraps

SERVES: 4 to 6 / PREP TIME: 20 minutes / COOK TIME: 10 minutes

Shrimp and avocado coated with a sweet sesame sauce in a crunchy lettuce cup will have you racing to the table. These cups have a kick from sriracha, a bit of tang from ginger, and zing from the fresh lime. Serve them with some warm steamed rice, cauliflower rice, Creamy Avocado Coleslaw (page 52), or your favorite fresh veggies. Or just wrap them up and devour them as is. If there are any leftovers, I think the shrimp might taste even better the next day. Try them cold over a bed of greens.

1 teaspoon olive oil

1 garlic clove, minced

1 teaspoon minced fresh ginger

1 pound large raw shrimp, peeled and deveined

2 tablespoons honey

1 tablespoon sesame oil

2 tablespoons gluten-free tamari or coconut aminos

2 tablespoons sriracha (optional)

CONTINUED >

1. In a large skillet, heat the oil over medium-high heat. Add the garlic and ginger and sauté, about 30 seconds or until fragrant. Add the shrimp and cook for 3 to 4 minutes, or until pink and cooked through.

2. In a large bowl, whisk together the honey, sesame oil, tamari, sriracha (if using), lime juice, and salt to taste. To that bowl, add the cooked shrimp, avocados, scallions, and carrots, and toss well to coat.

3. Divide the lettuce leaves between plates, or place them on a platter, and spoon the shrimp-and-avocado mixture into the center of each leaf (like a taco!). Top with the sesame seeds and serve with the lime wedges.

2 limes, one juiced, and
one sliced into wedges,
for serving

Sea salt

2 medium avocados, pitted,
peeled, and diced

2 scallions, green parts
only, chopped

1 large carrot, shredded

8 to 10 large butter lettuce
leaves (from 1 small head of
lettuce)

1 tablespoon toasted sesame
seeds, for garnish

 Shrimp cook quickly, so be sure to keep an eye on
them in the pan. In my experience, medium-high heat
for 3 minutes makes for the juiciest shrimp.

 If gluten isn't an issue, regular soy sauce can replace
the tamari or coconut aminos in equal measure.

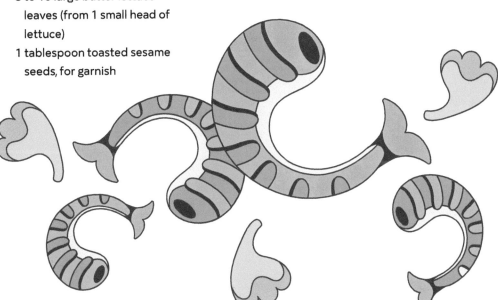

Pineapple-Lime Chutney and Salmon-Stuffed Avocados

SERVES: 4 / PREP TIME: 15 minutes / COOK TIME: 15 minutes

There are so many ways to stuff an avocado, but this one is by far my favorite. Gorgeous and good for you, this go-to dinner will be sure to turn heads and put a stop to hanger. Between the salmon's omega-3 fatty acids and the multitude of health benefits of avocado, the healthy meter on this recipe is beat only by its taste. I suggest using tamari or coconut aminos to keep this dish gluten-free, but traditional soy sauce can be used if gluten isn't an issue.

Grated zest and juice
  of 2 limes
2 tablespoons avocado oil or
  olive oil
2 tablespoons grated
  fresh ginger
2 tablespoons gluten-free
  tamari or coconut aminos
4 garlic cloves, minced
¼ cup chopped fresh parsley
Sea salt
Freshly ground black pepper
2 medium avocados, halved
  and pitted
2 (6-ounce) salmon fillets
½ cup diced fresh pineapple

1. In a large bowl, whisk together the lime zest and juice, oil, ginger, tamari, garlic, parsley, and salt and pepper to taste. Set aside.

2. Using a spoon, scoop out a portion of the avocado flesh to create a larger hole. You'll want to leave some avocado flesh on the sides and bottom of each half, but have enough room for your filling. Set the extra avocado flesh aside.

3. Dip the salmon fillets and avocado halves in the lime mixture and transfer to a foil-lined baking sheet. Broil on low for 8 minutes. Remove from the oven and set aside.

4. In a medium saucepan over medium heat, combine the pineapple and remaining lime mixture. Cook over medium heat for about 5 minutes until the liquid reduces slightly. Remove from heat and stir in the leftover avocado flesh. Add the salmon to the saucepan and flake the fish.

5. Stuff the 4 broiled avocado halves with the filling. Sprinkle with salt to taste.

 Not a fan of salmon or don't have any handy? Switch it up with canned tuna or even shredded chicken.

The Best Avo-Bean Burgers

SERVES: 4 / PREP TIME: 15 minutes, plus 15 minutes (or overnight) to chill /
COOK TIME: 15 minutes

Vegan or not, I truly believe this black bean burger could convince anyone to take a walk on the veg side. This plant-based patty is made with avocado, black beans, jalapeños, and oats and can certainly compete with its beefy counterparts. Stack them high with your favorite burger toppings like lettuce, onions, tomato, and cheese and your go-to condiments. I love my Spoon-Lickin' Roasted Garlic Guac (page 100) slathered on top.

1 medium avocado, pitted and peeled

3 tablespoons fresh lime juice

1 (15-ounce) can black beans, drained and rinsed, divided

¼ teaspoon garlic powder

¼ teaspoon sea salt

1 tablespoon chia seeds

¼ cup finely diced jalapeños

¼ cup chopped scallions, green parts only

¼ cup rolled oats

1 tablespoon olive oil

4 hamburger buns

1. In a medium bowl, mash the avocado and mix it with the lime juice. Add about half of the beans, the garlic powder, and salt. Mix until well combined. Add the chia seeds, jalapeños, green onions, oats, and remaining beans. Stir to combine completely.

2. Shape the mixture into 4 patties and refrigerate in a sealed container for at least 15 minutes or overnight.

3. When ready to cook, heat the oil in a large skillet over medium-high heat. Place the patties in the skillet, in batches if necessary, and cook for 5 to 7 minutes per side, until crispy and heated through. Serve on hamburger buns, topped with your favorite fixings.

These crowd-pleasing patties freeze well for a quick burger night. Once cooked, wrap each individually in plastic wrap and store in freezer-safe resealable bags for up to 3 months.

These burgers can easily be made gluten-free: Use gluten-free oats and your favorite gluten-free buns, or use the patties to top a salad.

Avocado, Corn, and Chicken Fritters with Zesty Lime Sour Cream

MAKES: 8 to 10 fritters / PREP TIME: 20 minutes / COOK TIME: 20 minutes

The fritter, a Southern favorite, actually has its origins in Native American cooking. No matter where they come from, be forewarned: These babies are avo-lutely delicious. The unique addition of avocado to the traditional chicken and corn adds flavor, color, and creaminess. When they're cooked just right, you'll find them crispy on the outside but soft in the middle.

1 cup sour cream

½ teaspoon grated lime zest

1 tablespoon fresh lime juice

Sea salt

½ pound boneless, skinless
   chicken thighs, diced in
   ⅓-inch-thick pieces

½ teaspoon paprika

½ teaspoon ground cumin

½ teaspoon ground ginger

Freshly ground black pepper

2 medium avocados, pitted,
   peeled, and diced

CONTINUED >

1. In a small bowl, stir together the sour cream, lime zest and juice, and salt to taste. Cover and refrigerate until ready to use.

2. Place the chicken a large mixing bowl. Mix in the paprika, cumin, and ginger. Season with salt and pepper and set aside.

3. Add the avocados and corn to the bowl with the chicken. If using canned corn, make sure it's been drained. Add the flour and baking powder and toss to coat. Add the eggs and dill. Stir in the bread crumbs, and let the mixture stand for 5 minutes. Line a plate with paper towels and set aside.

½ cup corn (fresh, frozen, or canned)

¼ cup all-purpose flour

1 tablespoon baking powder

2 large eggs, beaten

1 tablespoon chopped fresh dill

1 cup panko bread crumbs

2 cups olive oil, for frying

4. Heat the oil in a deep saucepan. When the oil is hot, scoop out ⅓ cup of the chicken-avocado mixture and gently add it to the oil in batches, slightly flattening out the top with the back of a spoon to form a patty. Fill the pan with as many patties as will fit, working in batches if necessary. Cook each patty for 2 to 3 minutes per side, until the outsides are golden brown and the chicken is fully cooked.

5. With a slotted spoon, remove the finished fritters to the plate to drain. Serve with the sour cream.

To test when your oil is hot enough to fry, flick a drop of water into the pan. If it sizzles, you're all set.

Prosciutto and Double-Cheese Pizza with Creamy Avocado Sauce

SERVES: 4 to 6 / PREP TIME: 15 minutes / COOK TIME: 15 minutes

Just when you thought pizza couldn't get any better, in walks the avocado. Along with smoky prosciutto, juicy tomatoes, and tangy red onion, avocado transforms pizza into a delicacy. Plus, making your own pizza is fun, fast and with boundless topping options, pleasing to every palate.

Nonstick cooking spray

1 (14-ounce) can refrigerated pizza dough

2 medium avocados, pitted, peeled, and sliced, divided

¼ cup lemon juice (from 1 to 2 lemons)

⅓ cup olive oil

2 garlic cloves, minced

½ cup fresh basil leaves

½ cup crème fraîche

Sea salt

Freshly ground black pepper

1 (6- to 8-ounce) log goat cheese, sliced, divided

CONTINUED >

1. Preheat the oven to 450°F. Lightly coat a 12-inch pizza pan or rimmed baking sheet with cooking spray.

2. Unroll the pizza dough, transfer it to the prepared pan, and press the dough to ⅛-inch thickness for thin crust, or ¼-inch thickness for thick-crust pizza.

3. In a blender, combine 1 avocado, the lemon juice, oil, garlic, basil, crème fraîche, and season with salt and pepper to taste. Puree until smooth. Use a spoon to spread the avocado sauce over the pizza dough.

4. Sprinkle half of the goat cheese and half the mozzarella over the avocado sauce. Add the arugula, tomato, and red onion. Then top with the prosciutto and the remaining sliced avocado. Finish by topping with the rest of the goat cheese and mozzarella. Bake for about 12 to 15 minutes, or until the cheese has melted.

1 cup shredded mozzarella
cheese, divided

1 cup arugula

1 small tomato, thinly sliced

1 red onion, thinly sliced

8 ounces prosciutto, sliced

 You can use your favorite kind of pizza dough here—just make sure to prepare and bake it according to the package or recipe directions. No dough at all? Pita bread works for a super-easy pizza crust, too.

 Play around with toppings or go halfsies with a picky partner. Fresh spinach and mushrooms work really well with this recipe.

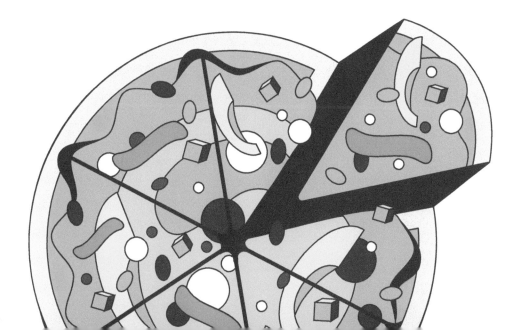

Mediterranean-Style Chicken Breasts with Tangy Avocado Tapenade

SERVES: 4 / PREP TIME: 30 minutes / COOK TIME: 20 minutes

When eating this bright, citrusy chicken, you'll imagine yourself sailing the Greek isles. The avocado tapenade with garlic, lemon, olives, and feta brings a bit of the Mediterranean in every bite. In this recipe, I use it to make boneless chicken breasts anything but boring, but it's great served with crackers or spooned over fish.

4 (6-ounce) boneless, skinless
   chicken breasts

1 tablespoon grated
   lemon zest

2 tablespoons fresh
   lemon juice

6 tablespoons olive
   oil, divided

1 garlic clove, finely chopped

Sea salt

Freshly ground black pepper

1 cup chopped yellow onion

2 tablespoons chopped
   fresh dill

CONTINUED >

1. In large bowl, combine the chicken breasts with the lemon zest and juice, 2 tablespoons of oil, and the garlic. Season with salt and pepper to taste. Cover and refrigerate for 30 minutes.

2. Meanwhile, in a large skillet over medium heat, heat 1 tablespoon of oil. Add the onion and cook for 8 minutes, stirring frequently, until softened. Remove the pan from the heat; stir in the dill, spinach, 1 cup of the Tangy Avocado Tapenade, and the feta. Let sit for 10 minutes.

3. When done marinating, remove the chicken from the refrigerator. Cut about a 3-inch-wide pocket into the thick side of each breast. Cut almost to the other side, but do not cut through completely. Stuff each pocket with the spinach mixture, and season with salt and pepper.

4 cups baby spinach

1 recipe Tangy Avocado Tapenade (page 99), divided

1 cup crumbled feta cheese, plus more for topping

6 tablespoons water

2 tablespoon pine nuts (optional)

4. In a large skillet over medium-high heat, heat 2 tablespoons of oil. Add the stuffed chicken, cover, and cook for 4 minutes. Then flip the chicken and reduce the heat to medium. Add the water to the pan, cover again, and cook until the chicken is browned and cooked through, about 10 minutes. The chicken should reach an internal temperature of 165°F and no longer be pink. Remove the chicken from the heat and let rest for at least 5 minutes.

5. Meanwhile, toast the pine nuts, if using. Put 1 tablespoon of oil in a small pan. Add the pine nuts and heat until lightly toasted, about 3 minutes per side. Plate the chicken and top with the toasted pine nuts, the remaining 1 cup of tapenade, and more feta, if desired.

Turkey, Cheddar, and Avocado Meatballs with Garlic Cauliflower Mash

SERVES: 4 / PREP TIME: 25 minutes / COOK TIME: 35 minutes

This full-flavored dish bursts with juicy turkey, sharp cheddar, fresh cilantro, and creamy avocado. When served over garlicky cauliflower mash, it's a definite winner of a dinner. Fix it to your preferences: Swap in ground chicken or beef, make some classic mashed potatoes, or try drizzling on your favorite sauce.

For the meatballs

1 pound ground turkey

1 large egg

½ cup shredded
   cheddar cheese

1 avocado, pitted, peeled,
   and mashed

½ cup minced yellow onion

1 tablespoon minced garlic

2 tablespoons finely chopped
   cilantro

1 teaspoon cayenne pepper

Sea salt

Freshly ground black pepper

Olive oil, for greasing

To make the meatballs

1. Preheat the oven to 350°F. Set a large pot of water to boil. Line a large baking sheet with aluminum foil.

2. In a large bowl, put the turkey, egg, cheese, avocado, onion, garlic, cilantro, and cayenne pepper. Season with salt and pepper to taste, and mix until thoroughly combined. Using a large tablespoon or ice cream scoop, create about 15 meatballs.

3. In a large saucepan over medium heat, heat the oil. Place the meatballs in the pan, and using tongs or a spoon, gently rotate the meatballs to cook for 4 minutes per side.

For the cauliflower mash

1 large head cauliflower, cut into florets

1 tablespoon olive oil

½ head garlic (about 6 cloves), minced

1 medium avocado, pitted, peeled, and mashed, or 3 ounces cream cheese, softened

Sea salt

Freshly ground black pepper

4. Once browned, remove the meatballs from the pan and place them on the foil-lined baking sheet, about 1 inch apart. Sprinkle with more salt and pepper, and bake for 10 minutes, until cooked through.

To make the cauliflower mash

5. While the meatballs are cooking, place a steamer basket in the pot of boiling water and add the cauliflower. Steam until tender, about 10 to 15 minutes.

6. In a small pan over medium-low heat, heat the oil. Add the garlic and cook, stirring to prevent burning, until slightly browned and soft, about 2 minutes. Remove from heat and set aside.

7. Once the cauliflower is very tender, transfer it to a blender or food processor. Add the garlic and the avocado and blend until creamy. You can also add everything to a pot or bowl and use an immersion blender. Taste, and season with salt and pepper. Serve the meatballs over the mashed cauliflower.

 Double the meatball recipe and freeze extras for later. Frozen cooked meatballs can last for up to 3 months and be cooked (thawed or unthawed) for 10 to 15 minutes. Frozen uncooked meatballs can last for up to 4 months, and should be cooked for 30 to 35 minutes.

Aji Verde Enchiladas

SERVES: 4 to 6 / PREP TIME: 30 minutes / COOK TIME: 1 hour

Enchiladas are top-tier Mexican cuisine, and in my book, this inspired recipe reigns supreme. These cheesy tortillas are stuffed with juicy chicken and smothered in a bright green Peruvian-inspired Aji Verde Sauce (page 94), a spicy avocado cream sauce, instead of the traditional mole. One bite and you'll know why these enchiladas wear the crown. Feel free to add cheddar to the mix or serve with diced onions.

2 pounds boneless, skinless chicken breasts

1 onion, halved, divided

Sea salt

½ cup fresh lime juice (from 3 to 4 limes)

2 teaspoons ground cumin

2 garlic cloves

2 cups Aji Verde Sauce (page 94), divided

12 (8-inch) corn tortillas

Olive oil, to rub on tortillas

2 cups queso fresco

Sour cream, for serving

1 bunch fresh cilantro, chopped, for serving

1. In a large pot, place the chicken with half of the onion and salt and cover with water. Bring to a boil and reduce the heat to simmer until cooked through, about 20 minutes. Remove the chicken from the water, shred it, and add it back to the pot.

2. Mince the remaining half of the onion and add it to the pot, along with the lime juice, cumin, garlic, and 1 cup of the aji verde sauce. Season with salt to taste. Heat the pot over low for 15 to 20 minutes.

3. Preheat the oven to 350°F. Line a baking sheet with aluminum foil. Rub the tortillas with oil on both sides, and bake for 2 minutes per side, until soft and lightly browned.

4. Place one of the tortillas in a 9-by-13-inch casserole dish. Using a slotted spoon, scoop approximately 2 tablespoons of the chicken mixture onto the tortilla and roll tightly. Place it seam-side down. Repeat with the remaining tortillas and chicken, keeping them in a single layer.

5. Cover the enchiladas with the remaining cup of aji verde sauce and sprinkle with the queso fresco. Transfer the dish to the oven and bake until the cheese is melted, about 15 minutes. Remove from the oven and serve with sour cream and cilantro.

 In a time crunch? Use store-bought salsa verde in place of the aji verde sauce. Just blend it with some jalapeño (depending on how much heat you want) and an avocado to create the creamy texture.

Eggplant Parmesan with Creamy Avocado Pesto

SERVES: 6 / PREP TIME: 20 minutes / COOK TIME: 1 hour

This Italian classic gets an avocado enhancement. Here, the sliced roasted eggplant you already love is smothered with a garlicky basil pesto that's made smooth and creamy by our favorite green fruit. To make this dish vegetarian, replace the Parmesan with even more mozzarella.

3 cups marinara sauce

½ cup Creamy Avocado Pesto (page 96)

1 teaspoon dried oregano

4 garlic cloves, minced

½ teaspoon red pepper flakes

2 medium eggplants, sliced into ¼-inch-thick rounds

1 tablespoon olive oil

Sea salt

Freshly ground black pepper

2 cups shredded mozzarella cheese

1 cup grated Parmesan cheese

Chopped fresh basil, for topping

1. Preheat the oven to 375°F. In a medium saucepan, combine the marinara sauce, pesto, oregano, garlic, and red pepper. Cook over medium-low heat for 10 minutes, stirring frequently. Set aside.

2. Line a baking sheet with parchment paper and arrange the eggplant rounds in a single layer. Brush with the oil and season with salt and pepper. Roast for about 25 minutes, flipping halfway through, until slightly browned. Remove from the oven and set aside.

3. In a 9-by-13-inch casserole dish, spread 1 cup of the marinara mixture. Add a layer of eggplant, then another layer of marinara sauce, followed by a layer of mozzarella and Parmesan. Do another layer of the remaining eggplant, the remaining marinara sauce, and the remaining cheeses. Bake for 20 to 25 minutes, until the cheese has begun to brown. Serve topped with the fresh basil.

Afraid of mushy, bitter eggplants? Try salting them first. Sprinkling raw slices of eggplant with salt will help draw out the bitter liquid. Lightly salt, let sit for a few minutes, then rinse and dry before you cook.

Next-Level Broccoli-and-Cheese Casserole

SERVES: 8 / PREP TIME: 10 minutes / COOK TIME: 20 minutes

Introducing a modern take on the broccoli and cheese casserole of your childhood! Made with fresh broccoli, creamy avocado, two kinds of cheese, and a buttery, crunchy topping, it's a decadent dish that blows other versions away. It's perfect for a night when you really need some comfort food but still want to be fancy.

2 tablespoons butter, plus more for greasing

Sea salt

6 cups fresh broccoli florets

2 avocados, pitted, peeled, and mashed

1 (8-ounce) package cream cheese, softened

1½ cups grated cheddar cheese

½ cup grated Parmesan cheese

3 garlic cloves, minced

Freshly ground black pepper

1 cup crushed buttery crackers, such as Ritz

1. Preheat the oven to 350°F. Grease a 9-by-13-inch baking dish with butter and set aside.

2. In a large saucepan, bring ½ inch of salted water to a boil. Add the broccoli, cover, and cook over high heat until crisp-tender, about 3 to 4 minutes. Drain, and transfer the broccoli to the prepared baking dish. Set aside while you prepare the cheese sauce.

3. In a large mixing bowl, put the avocados, cream cheese, cheddar, and Parmesan, leaving a bit of each cheese aside for topping. Add the garlic and butter and mix until thoroughly combined. Season with salt and pepper.

4. Stir in the broccoli and mix well. Transfer the mixture to the baking dish, and top with the remaining cheese and the crushed crackers. Bake for 15 to 20 minutes, or until lightly browned on top.

5. Remove from the oven and let stand 5 minutes before serving. Any leftovers will last in a covered container in the fridge for up to 3 days.

My grandmother made this with canned cream of broccoli soup, and so can you. For this retro twist, just swap it for half of the cream cheese. You can also use bread crumbs in place of the crackers, but the topping won't be as crunchy.

Frozen broccoli florets work here, too. Just make sure to thaw and drain them before using.

Avocado Toast: Main Dish Edition

Make your toast the main event with these hearty palate pleasers.

Parma Avocado Baguette

Take a tour of Italy in one bite with this avocado eggplant Parm.

 A halved and toasted baguette topped with marinara sauce, sliced roasted eggplant, and sliced avocado, and sprinkled with Parmesan and garlic salt.

Buffalo Blue Cheese Avocado Toast

This kickin' chicken is a toast above the rest with creamy avocado and bold blue cheese, all covered in hot sauce to turn up the heat.

 Sliced grilled chicken breast on brioche topped with sliced avocado, sprinkled with blue cheese, and covered with spicy Buffalo sauce.

Chapter 6

DIPS, SPREADS & CONDIMENTS

GLUTEN-FREE, 30 MINUTES OR LESS, VEGETARIAN

Aji Verde Sauce

MAKES: about 2 cups / PREP TIME: 5 minutes

Meet your new favorite green sauce. This bold and bright take on a classic Peruvian dip is zesty, tangy, and packed with fresh flavor. A drizzle of aji verde makes the most basic of foods taste irresistible. Chicken, tacos, eggs, rice and beans, potatoes, and more! I love spice and have been known to use up to four jalapeños for this sauce, so feel free to experiment until you find your perfect number.

2 medium jalapeños, chopped

1 medium avocado, pitted
    and peeled

1 cup fresh cilantro

4 garlic cloves

1 tablespoon avocado oil or
    olive oil

½ cup mayonnaise or
    Greek yogurt

⅓ cup grated cotija cheese

2 tablespoons fresh
    lime juice

⅓ cup water

Sea salt

1. In a blender or food processor, combine the jalapeños, avocado, cilantro, garlic, oil, mayonnaise, cheese, lime juice, and water. Blend on high speed until a smooth sauce forms. Taste and season with salt, if needed. If the sauce is too thick, add more water. You'll want to be able to pour it easily . . . on everything!

2. Transfer the sauce to a container with a tight-fitting lid. It will last in the refrigerator for up to a week.

 Cotija, a hard, crumbly Mexican cow's-milk cheese, gives this sauce its most authentic taste. You can find it in most cheese aisles. It most closely resembles feta. If you're not worried about keeping this sauce vegetarian, you can use Parmesan instead.

Avocado Blanco Dip

MAKES: about 2 cups / PREP TIME: 5 minutes, plus 3 to 5 hours to chill

This creamy, garlicky sauce is *addiptive*! With a little bit of sweetness and a lot of spice, it's the perfect pairing for a chip and veggie platter—though I suspect you'll find yourself putting it on everything. For a bolder heat, increase the amounts of red pepper flakes and cayenne pepper to ½ teaspoon. It's easier to up the heat quotient than to cool it down. Keep in mind that the magic to this sauce is refrigeration. The longer it chills, the more delicious it gets.

1 medium avocado, pitted and peeled

2 cups Greek yogurt

6 garlic cloves, minced

½ teaspoon garlic powder

¼ teaspoon red pepper flakes

¼ teaspoon cayenne pepper

½ cup sugar

½ teaspoon sea salt

1 teaspoon ground cumin

1 teaspoon dried oregano

Juice of 1 lime

1. In a blender or food processor, combine the avocado, yogurt, garlic cloves and powder, red pepper flakes, cayenne pepper, sugar, salt, cumin, oregano, and lime juice. Blend on high speed until a smooth dip forms. If the dip is too thick, add water until you reach your desired consistency.

2. Transfer it to a container with a lid and refrigerate for 3 to 5 hours before serving. Technically, it will store in the refrigerator for 2 to 3 days, but it never lasts that long in my house!

 This recipe uses Greek yogurt, but feel free to use mayo if you prefer it.

Creamy Avocado Pesto

MAKES: about 2 cups / PREP TIME: 10 minutes / COOK TIME: 5 minutes

If you think pesto is perfect as it is, hold on to your taste buds. Add a little avocado and you've created a creamier, richer, *greener* spread that any nonna would be proud to throw on her pasta. Toss it over warm linguine, spread it on a crunchy baguette, or use it to top your eggs.

¼ cup pine nuts

½ cup grated pecorino cheese

½ cup grated
Parmesan cheese

4 garlic cloves

2 cups fresh basil

1 cup baby spinach

2 medium avocados, pitted
and peeled

Juice of 1 lemon

½ cup avocado oil or
olive oil

Sea salt

Freshly ground black pepper

1. Preheat the oven to 350°F.

2. Place the pine nuts on a baking sheet and roast for 5 minutes, until lightly toasted.

3. In blender or food processer bowl, combine the pine nuts, pecorino and Parmesan cheeses, and garlic and pulse until finely ground.

4. Add the basil, spinach, avocado, and lemon juice. With the food processor on low, slowly add the oil until the pesto reaches your desired consistency. Taste, and season with salt and pepper as needed.

5. Transfer the pesto to a jar with a lid or an airtight container, and store in the refrigerator for up to a week.

Swap out the cheeses for 1 cup of nutritional yeast to create a vegan, plant-based alternative pesto. Or trade in the pine nuts for any hard nut, like almonds or walnuts.

 Making pesto ice cubes is a great way to freeze pesto for later use. Spoon the pesto into ice cube trays, freeze, and then pop the cubes into a freezer-safe resealable bag. They'll last for about 3 months.

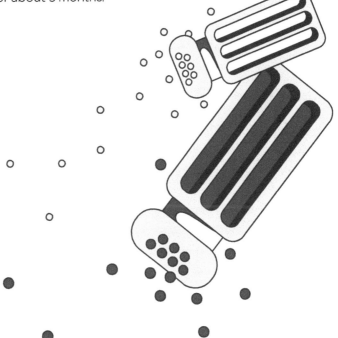

Jalapeño and Avocado Hummus

MAKES: about 2 cups / PREP TIME: 5 minutes

This recipe brings chickpeas and avocado together to create what I consider the most amazing dip duo of all time. This inspired bit of Mexican and Mediterranean fusion combines everything you love about guacamole and hummus into one hard-to-stop-eating dip. Let your taste buds be your guide when it comes to the jalapeños. Increase (or decrease) at your own risk! To serve, sprinkle on some roasted pumpkin seeds or pepitas for crunch and flair.

2 medium avocados, pitted
  and peeled
2 (15-ounce) cans chickpeas,
  drained and rinsed
4 garlic cloves
2 jalapeño peppers, seeded
  and diced, divided
Juice of 1 lime
½ cup fresh cilantro
1 teaspoon ground cumin
Sea salt
Freshly ground black pepper
2 tablespoons avocado oil
  or olive oil, plus more for
  drizzling
¼ cup water
¼ cup crumbled feta cheese
  (optional)

1. In a blender or food processor, combine the avocados, chickpeas, garlic, about ¾ of the diced jalapeños, lime juice, cilantro, cumin, salt and pepper to taste, oil, and water. Blend until a smooth dip forms. Taste and adjust the seasonings as needed.

2. Transfer to a bowl and drizzle with more oil. Top with the remaining jalapeño, feta, if using, and sea salt. Refrigerate in an airtight container for up to 3 days.

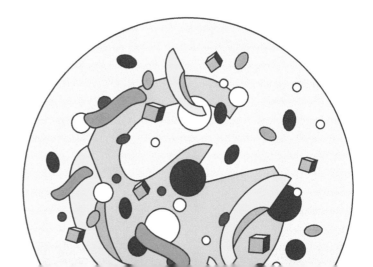

Tangy Avocado Tapenade

MAKES: about 2 cups / PREP TIME: 15 minutes

Tapenade is a Provençal name for a dish that consists of pureed or finely chopped olives. That's all well and good, but obviously I had to up the ante here by adding some avocado. This briny spread is incredibly easy to make and adds so much flavor to a dish. It's great to level up your crackers, sandwiches, and yes, avocado toast.

1 medium avocado, pitted, peeled, and finely diced

1 cup black olives, pitted and chopped

1 cup green olives, pitted and chopped

1 tablespoon capers

½ tablespoon chopped fresh parsley

½ tablespoon chopped fresh basil

2 anchovies, chopped (optional)

1 garlic clove, minced

½ cup avocado oil or olive oil

1 tablespoon fresh lemon juice

Sea salt

Freshly ground black pepper

In a medium bowl, put the avocado, black and green olives, capers, parsley, basil, anchovies, if using, garlic, oil, and lemon juice. Mix together until well combined. Season with salt and pepper. Transfer to an airtight container and store in the refrigerator for up to 3 days.

LP's Spoon-Lickin' Roasted Garlic Guac

MAKES: about 2 cups / PREP TIME: 10 minutes / COOK TIME: 1 hour, plus 10 minutes to cool

Everyone's gotta have a go-to guacamole recipe. Some people swear by just adding lime juice, others add tomatoes, and then there are those who add peas! Any way you make it, this iconic dip is always a hit. My version, with its lime juice and fresh cilantro, is close to the classic but with a super-savory spin: *a lot* of roasted garlic.

4 heads garlic

2 tablespoons olive oil

4 large avocados, pitted and peeled

1 cup minced red onion

¼ cup fresh lime juice (from about 2 limes)

¼ teaspoon cayenne pepper

¼ cup chopped fresh cilantro

Sea salt

Freshly ground black pepper

¼ cup queso fresco, for serving (optional)

¼ cup pepitas, for serving (optional)

1. Preheat the oven to 450°F.

2. Slice off the tops of the heads of garlic and place each one in the center of a piece of foil. Drizzle each with the oil and tightly wrap the foil around them. Place the foil packets on the center rack of the oven and roast for 45 minutes to 1 hour. Remove from the oven, carefully unwrap the foil, and check to see if the garlic is done. If it's not soft and mushy, put it back in the oven for a few more minutes. Once roasted, let the garlic cool for at least 10 minutes.

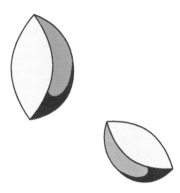

3. While the garlic is cooling, in a large bowl, combine the avocados and onion. Using a spoon, add the roasted garlic cloves to the bowl. Mash the mixture with a fork or potato masher a few times. Add the lime juice and cayenne pepper and mash the mixture until smooth but still chunky. Season with salt and pepper. Serve with the queso fresco and pepitas, if using. Store covered in the refrigerator for up to 2 days.

 There are so many ways to mix up this dip. Sweeten it with some diced mango or a drizzle of honey. More savory add-ins include Parmesan or pesto. You could *really* lean into your obsession and double the avo with the addition of some Creamy Avocado Pesto (page 96). Be creative; the combinations are endless!

 The secret to keeping your guac green may sound wild, but trust me. Put your guac in an airtight container, pour 1/2 inch of water on top, cover, and refrigerate. Pour the water off before serving—and be amazed.

Rosemary-Avocado Compound Butter

MAKES: About 1 cup / PREP TIME: 10 minutes, plus 1 hour to chill

I can't believe it's avocado . . . butter? That's right. The traditional churned spread gets a delectable infusion of lemon and rosemary and the creamy addition of avocado. This butter is perfect to spread on toast, toss on roasted potatoes, or melt over grilled fish or steak.

1 medium avocado, pitted and peeled

½ cup unsalted butter, softened

1½ teaspoons fresh lemon juice

1 garlic clove

½ teaspoon fresh rosemary

Sea salt

Freshly ground black pepper

1. Line a baking sheet or large plate with parchment paper.

2. In a blender or food processor, combine the avocado, butter, lemon juice, garlic, rosemary, and salt and pepper to taste and blend until a smooth spread forms.

3. Scoop the mixture onto the parchment paper and roll it up to form a cylinder. Twist both ends tight, and refrigerate for at least one hour. The butter is ready to serve when cold and solid, and will last in the refrigerator for about five days.

 Use any fresh herbs you have on hand, like dill, thyme, or basil. This butter can also be stored in an airtight container in the freezer for 6 to 9 months.

Strawberry-Avocado Jam

MAKES: about 1 cup / PREP TIME: 5 minutes / COOK TIME: 15 minutes

This isn't your grandma's strawberry preserves. Fresh strawberries, chunky avocado, and crunchy chia seeds come together to make an unparalleled biscuit topping. Not only do the chia seeds help the jam thicken up without loads of sugar or thickeners like pectin, but they are also a superfood, packing tons of fiber, protein, and omega-3 fatty acids into just a spoonful. You can make this jam with any of your favorite fruits. Try mangos or raspberries for a different flavor.

2 cups diced fresh
   strawberries

2 tablespoons
   balsamic vinegar

2 tablespoons fresh
   lemon juice

1 cup granulated sugar or
   2 tablespoons maple syrup

1 medium avocado, pitted,
   peeled, and diced

2 tablespoons chia seeds

1. In a medium saucepan over medium heat, combine the strawberries, vinegar, lemon juice, and sugar. Cook, stirring frequently, until the mixture comes to a boil. Reduce the heat to low and stir in the avocado and chia seeds. Let it simmer, stirring occasionally, for about 10 minutes, or until the jam has thickened.

2. Remove the pan from the heat. The jam will continue to thicken as it cools. Transfer to a container with a tight-fitting lid and refrigerate for up to a week.

 You can use frozen strawberries in this recipe. Thaw and dice them before adding to the saucepan.

 Honey will work as a sweetener here; just note that the recipe will no longer be vegan.

Avocado Hollandaise

MAKES: about 2 cups / **PREP TIME:** 10 minutes

Not in fact from Holland, this luscious, rich *French* sauce gets a healthy reimagining here with this velvety, creamy puree of avocado and lemon juice. This vegan version of the brunchtime staple is super simple and delicious. Pour the sauce over eggs, asparagus, or potatoes for a rich twist to any dish.

1 medium avocado, pitted
  and peeled
Juice of 1 lemon
⅓ cup hot water
¼ cup olive oil
Sea salt
Freshly ground black pepper
Dash of cayenne pepper
  (optional)
Red pepper flakes (optional)

1. In a blender or food processor, combine the avocado, lemon juice, and hot water. Puree until smooth and fluffy, about 2 minutes.

2. With the blender on low, drizzle in the oil and blend until combined, adding more water if the mixture is too thick. Taste and season with salt and pepper as needed. Add the cayenne pepper and/or red pepper flakes, if using. Transfer to a jar or airtight container and store in the refrigerator for up to 2 days.

Chapter 7

DRINKS & DESSERTS

Frozen Avo-Rita

MAKES: 2 drinks / PREP TIME: 5 minutes

Have you ever been eating an avocado and thought, *This needs some tequila*? Oh, just me? Regardless, this cocktail will satisfy a need you either knew or didn't know you had. The mild and buttery flavor of the avocado mixed with the kick of the tequila, the sweetness of the agave, and the freshness of the cilantro creates a silky, refreshing drink you'll be sipping all summer long.

1 medium avocado, pitted and peeled

2 cups ice

4 ounces tequila

2 ounces orange juice

2 ounces fresh lime juice

3 teaspoons agave nectar

¼ cup fresh cilantro, chopped

1 jalapeño, sliced (optional)

2 tablespoons coarse sea salt

2 teaspoons grated lime zest

1 lime, cut into wedges

Pinch cayenne pepper (optional)

1. In a blender, combine the avocado, ice, tequila, orange juice, lime juice, agave nectar, cilantro, and jalapeño, if using. Puree until smooth.

2. On a small plate, sprinkle the salt and lime zest. Rub the rim of each glass with a lime wedge and dip it into the salt-lime mixture.

3. Pour the drink into the glasses, and top with the cayenne pepper, if using, and lime wedges to serve.

 Make it a mocktail! Nondrinkers can join in on the fun by replacing the tequila with sparkling water. Honey can also replace the agave nectar, but the drink will no longer be vegan.

 I've found that silver or blanco tequila works best with this recipe.

GLUTEN-FREE, NUT-FREE, 30 MINUTES OR LESS, VEGETARIAN

Avo-Citrus Smoothie

MAKES: 2 smoothies / PREP TIME: 5 minutes

Add some sunshine to your morning routine with this citrus smoothie simply packed with vitamin C and fiber, and antioxidants from the avocado. The quick prep will keep you on time, and one sip is bound to get you moving in the ripe direction!

1 banana, sliced

1 large orange, peeled, seeded, and segmented

½ grapefruit, peeled, seeded, and segmented

1 medium avocado, pitted and peeled

2 teaspoons honey

1 cup milk

6 ice cubes

1. In a blender, combine the banana, orange, grapefruit, avocado, honey, milk, and ice.

2. Blend on high until creamy and smooth. If the smoothie is too thick, add more milk; if too thin, add more banana or avocado.

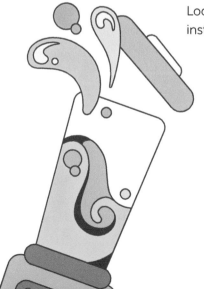

This recipe is a versatile and healthy one. You can use any variety of citrus you love and add in superfoods like turmeric or chia seeds for an extra health boost. Looking for a vegan variation? Use agave nectar instead of honey and a plant-based milk.

Creamy Avocado Ice Pops

MAKES: 8 to 10 ice pops / PREP TIME: 10 minutes, plus 8 hours to freeze

The very first "Popsicle" was invented by accident by an 11-year-old boy. But this treat is no mistake. This variety is a Filipino favorite, traditionally called "ice candy" for its unique mix of sweet-and-savory-meets-cold-and-creamy. This method uses the ice pop tubes that can be found at specialty stores, but regular ice pop molds will work as well.

2 cups full-fat coconut milk

1 cup water

½ cup honey

4 medium avocados, pitted and peeled

1. In a blender, combine the coconut milk, water, honey, and avocados and blend until smooth.

2. Using a funnel (or good aim), slowly pour the avocado mixture into the ice pop tubes. Seal them according to the product directions.

3. Freeze for at least 8 hours. These will last in the freezer for up to 3 months.

 You can add in more flavor like a few fresh mint leaves or a drop of vanilla extract, or try it with some pureed fruit, such as melon, pineapple, or mango.

DAIRY-FREE, GLUTEN-FREE, VEGETARIAN

Avocado, Date, and Nut Truffles

MAKES: 16 truffles / PREP TIME: 15 minutes, plus 30 minutes to chill

Congratulations! Candy essentially just became part of your well-balanced diet. These avocado-and-date truffles are a guilt-free way to satisfy your sweet tooth. You can do so much with these truffles: Switch up the nuts, dip them in chocolate, or roll them in powdered sugar or sprinkles. Your imagination is the limit.

1 cup unsalted, raw or roasted whole pistachios, plus ¼ cup finely chopped, for rolling

¼ cup unsweetened shredded coconut

1 cup unsalted, raw or roasted whole walnuts

1 cup pitted dates

1 medium avocado, pitted, peeled, and diced

2 tablespoons honey

¼ cup coconut oil

½ tablespoon vanilla extract

½ cup unsweetened cocoa powder

Sea salt

1. Cover a baking sheet with parchment paper and set aside. Place the chopped pistachios and shredded coconut in a medium bowl and stir to combine. Set aside.

2. In a blender or food processer, combine the whole pistachios and walnuts and pulse until finely chopped, 1 to 2 minutes.

3. Add the dates, avocado, honey, coconut oil, vanilla, cocoa powder, and a pinch of salt, and continue to blend until a dough forms. Roll pieces of the dough into about 16 silver-dollar-size balls.

4. Roll the dough balls in the coconut-and-pistachio mixture to coat. Place the finished truffles on the prepared baking sheet, then sprinkle with sea salt to taste. Refrigerate for 30 minutes before serving. Truffles can be stored in the refrigerator for up to a week.

 For vegan truffles, replace the honey with maple syrup or agave.

Mango, Raspberry, and Avocado Cupcakes

MAKES: 12 cupcakes / PREP TIME: 25 minutes / COOK TIME: 20 minutes

These fruity cupcakes leave basic vanilla in the dust, creating a trifecta of flavor, color, and yes, nutrients. The combo of raspberries, mango, and avocado makes for a moist and delicious treat that hits the sweet spot. These are amazing topped with Strawberry-Avocado Jam (page 103).

1½ cups all-purpose flour

1½ teaspoons
   baking powder

½ teaspoon baking soda

¼ teaspoon sea salt

1 medium avocado, pitted
   and peeled

¾ cup granulated sugar

2 medium eggs

1 teaspoon vanilla extract

1 cup Greek yogurt

¾ cup vegetable oil

1 cup finely diced mango

1 cup raspberries

Juice of 1 lime

1. Preheat the oven to 350°F. Line a 12-cup muffin pan with baking cups.

2. In a medium bowl, stir together the flour, baking powder, baking soda, and salt. In a large bowl, mash the avocado until smooth.

3. Add the sugar and eggs to the avocado and beat with an electric mixer or by hand until completely combined, about 5 to 7 minutes. Add the vanilla, yogurt, and oil and mix until smooth.

4. Stir in the mango, raspberries, and lime juice, and then slowly stir the flour mixture in to the batter, in two parts, mixing until combined.

5. Spoon the batter into the muffin cups. Bake for 20 minutes or until a toothpick inserted into the center comes out clean. Store cupcakes in an airtight container for up to 3 days.

 I find fresh fruit works best in this recipe, but in a pinch you can use frozen mango or raspberries. Thaw the fruit and drain off any excess liquid before using.

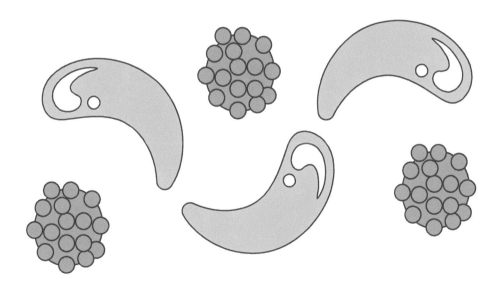

Key Lime and Avocado Pie

SERVES: 12 / PREP TIME: 5 minutes / COOK TIME: 10 minutes, plus 5 hours to chill

This summer staple was already green and creamy, but now it's greener and creamier. In addition to its gorgeous hue, avocado enhances the key lime pie texture you already love. After it's poured into a buttery graham cracker crust and topped with fresh whipped cream and a lime twist garnish, it'll transport you to the Florida Keys. If you have leftover heavy cream from making the filling, use it to make homemade whipped cream.

For the crust

Nonstick cooking spray

1½ cups graham
cracker crumbs

¼ cup sugar

Pinch sea salt

4 tablespoons unsalted
butter, melted

For the filling

1½ cups heavy cream

12 ounces cream cheese,
softened

¾ cup sugar

Pinch sea salt

3 medium avocados, pitted,
peeled, and diced

CONTINUED >

To make the crust

1. Preheat the oven to 350°F. Spray a 9-inch pie dish with nonstick cooking spray and set aside.

2. In a large bowl, combine the graham cracker crumbs, sugar, salt, and melted butter and mix until combined. Press the graham cracker mixture firmly into the prepared dish. Bake for 8 to 10 minutes, until toasted. Remove and let cool to room temperature.

To make the filling and assemble

3. Into a large bowl, pour the heavy cream. Use an electric mixer and mix on high speed until stiff peaks form. In a separate bowl, beat the cream cheese, sugar, and salt until smooth and fluffy, about 3 minutes. Add the avocados and beat until smooth.

4. Put the avocado mixture into a food processor, add the lime juice and zest, and blend until smooth. Add in the whipped cream and pulse until smooth and thick.

Juice and grated zest from
  5 Key limes

Whipped cream, for garnish
  (optional)

1 lime, sliced into rounds, for
  garnish (optional)

5. Transfer the filling to the cooled pie crust. Garnish with dollops of whipped cream and lime slices, if desired. Chill until solid, about 4 to 5 hours, then serve.

 Can't find Key limes? You can make this recipe with regular limes.

 If you don't have an electric mixer, use a hand whisk to get the heavy cream fluffy or even try the lowest setting on a blender.

Papaya and Avocado Panna Cotta

SERVES: 6 / PREP TIME: 10 minutes, plus 5 hours to chill / COOK TIME: 15 minutes

Panna cotta, meaning "thick cream," comes from Italy. Here we give the traditional dessert a taste of the islands to make a showstopping fruit-filled chilled custard. The papaya pairs perfectly with the avocado, and its sweetness mellows out the heat from the chili powder, so don't be afraid of the spice.

1 (15-ounce) can full-fat coconut milk, divided

1½ teaspoons unflavored gelatin

4 teaspoons honey, divided

1 teaspoon vanilla extract

1 medium avocado, pitted, peeled, and mashed

½ cup fresh or frozen papaya

1 teaspoon fresh lemon juice

1 teaspoon chili powder (optional)

1. In a medium saucepan over medium heat, heat 1 cup of the coconut milk with the gelatin. Stir and let sit until the gelatin begins to soften, about 10 minutes.

2. To the same pan, add the remaining coconut milk and 2 teaspoons honey. Bring to a boil over medium-high heat, whisking frequently, about 5 minutes. Remove the pan from the heat, add the vanilla and let cool, about 15 minutes.

3. In a blender, combine the cooled coconut milk mixture with the avocado and pulse until smooth.

4. Pour the blended mixture into serving dishes. Cover each dish with plastic wrap and transfer to the refrigerator for 4 to 5 hours or until the panna cotta has set.

5. In a small saucepan, bring the papaya, remaining honey, and lemon juice to a boil, then reduce heat to simmer for 10 minutes. Remove from the heat and let cool.

6. When ready to serve, top the panna cotta with the papaya compote and sprinkle with chili powder, if using.

Gelatin is a thickening agent that can be found in the baking section of your local grocery store. Although most brands of gelatin are not vegetarian or vegan, agar agar is, if you want to use that and replace the honey with agave nectar.

Avo love: Avocado trees need another avocado tree close by in order to grow.

Avocado and Almond Butter Chocolate Chip Cookies

MAKES: 12 cookies / PREP TIME: 5 minutes / COOK TIME: 10 minutes

I might go out on a limb and claim that these cookies are good for you—at the very least, they'll make you happy! This recipe begs to be experimented with: If you don't have a dairy allergy, try your favorite type of chocolate. Allergic to nuts? Try sunflower seed butter instead. You can even make these with a crunchy nut butter for some texture. For a vegan option, you can replace the honey with agave nectar.

1 large avocado, pitted, peeled, and mashed
2/3 cup almond butter
1 large egg
1/4 cup honey
1/2 teaspoon baking powder
1/2 cup dairy-free dark chocolate chips
Flaky sea salt, for garnish (optional)

1. Preheat the oven to 375°F. Line a baking sheet with parchment paper and set aside.

2. In a large bowl, put the avocado, almond butter, egg, and honey. Using an electric mixer, mix on medium speed until well combined. Slowly add the baking powder and mix. Fold in the chocolate chips using a spatula or spoon.

3. Scoop out about 2 tablespoons of dough, roll it into a ball, and place it on the prepared baking sheet. Repeat until all the dough is used, keeping the cookies evenly spaced on the baking sheet. With a fork, flatten the top of each cookie slightly in a crisscross pattern.

4. Bake for 8 to 10 minutes, until the edges are crisp. Remove from the oven and immediately transfer the cookies to a cooling rack. Sprinkle with salt, if using. These will last for a week stored in an airtight container at room temperature.

Avocado Toast: Dessert Edition

Avocado toast does not discriminate. It takes on all of the day's meals, including dessert. Try these for some sweet after-dinner treats.

Sweet and Creamy Brie and Avocado Sweet Potato Toast with Walnuts

Turn a boring piece of sweet potato into a decadent and delicious toast topped with melty Brie and honey for a treat that's both pretty and sweet!

 Sliced and roasted sweet potato topped with melted Brie and sliced avocado, drizzled with honey, and sprinkled with chopped walnuts.

Chocolate-Hazelnut, Banana, and Avocado Graham Crackers

These sweet and savory graham crackers are loaded with creamy avocado and hazelnut spread for a dessert that will have you asking for seconds.

 Graham crackers topped with chocolate-hazelnut spread, sliced avocado, sliced bananas, and a pinch of cinnamon.

MEASUREMENT CONVERSIONS

Volume Equivalents

	U.S. STANDARD	U.S. STANDARD (OUNCES)	METRIC (APPROXIMATE)
Liquid	2 tablespoons	1 fl. oz.	30 mL
	¼ cup	2 fl. oz.	60 mL
	½ cup	4 fl. oz.	120 mL
	1 cup	8 fl. oz.	240 mL
	1½ cups	12 fl. oz.	355 mL
	2 cups or 1 pint	16 fl. oz.	475 mL
	4 cups or 1 quart	32 fl. oz.	1 L
	1 gallon	128 fl. oz.	4 L
Dry	⅛ teaspoon	—	0.5 mL
	¼ teaspoon	—	1 mL
	½ teaspoon	—	2 mL
	¾ teaspoon	—	4 mL
	1 teaspoon	—	5 mL
	1 tablespoon	—	15 mL
	¼ cup	—	59 mL
	⅓ cup	—	79 mL
	½ cup	—	118 mL
	⅔ cup	—	156 mL
	¾ cup	—	177 mL
	1 cup	—	235 mL
	2 cups or 1 pint	—	475 mL
	3 cups	—	700 mL
	4 cups or 1 quart	—	1 L
	½ gallon	—	2 L
	1 gallon	—	4 L

Oven Temperatures

FAHRENHEIT	CELSIUS (APPROX)
250°F	120°C
300°F	150°C
325°F	165°C
350°F	180°C
375°F	190°C
400°F	200°C
425°F	220°C
450°F	230°C

Weight Equivalents

U.S. STANDARD	METRIC (APPROX)
½ ounce	15 g
1 ounce	30 g
2 ounces	60 g
4 ounces	115 g
8 ounces	225 g
12 ounces	340 g
16 ounces or 1 pound	455 g

INDEX

ACKNOWLEDGMENTS

Love and endless appreciation to all the beautiful women in my family, for the memories I made and life lessons I learned in your kitchens.

Gratitude to my brilliant editor, Gleni Bartels, for this amazing avo-tunity.

And to all of you out there cooking up change in this world, thank you.

ABOUT THE AUTHOR

Lauren Paige Richeson is a recipe developer, photographer, and lifestyle content creator.

She's the brains behind the website LPFEDME.com, a dreamy escape into equal parts home cooking and world exploration, where she crafts simple, healthy yet hearty recipes that are "one cup Julia Child + a dash of Beyoncé." Through her platform she aims to encourage the belief "Living well isn't a luxury. It's a lifestyle." You can follow along with her adventures on her Instagram @lpfedme.